MW01643609

LEONARDO

By: MINA BACCI

AVENEL BOOKS
NEW YORK

First U.S. Edition published 1978 by Avenel Books
distributed by Crown Publishers Inc.
Printed in Italy by Fabbri Editori, Milan.
a b c d e f g h i

Library of Congress Cataloging in Publication Data
Leonardo da Vinci, 1452-1519.
Leonardo.
1. Leonardo da Vinci, 1452-1519. I. Bacci, Mina. II. Title.
ND623.L5A4 1978 759.5 78-18879
ISBN 0-517-24952-9

Leonardo, the illegitimate son of Master Piero, a public notary, and of a certain Caterina, was born in Vinci in 1452. When Leonardo was 17 his father moved to Florence, where Leonardo entered the workshop of Verrocchio. There, he stood out among the apprentices due to his father's social status, his better cultural background, his unique personality, and especially his unquestionable ability to paint. This is confirmed by Vasari's story of Verrocchio's indignation when he saw that Leonardo, his student, had surpassed him in painting the figure of the angel in Baptism of Christ *(Uffizi) and that "he (Verrocchio) never wanted to touch colors again."*

In 1472 Leonardo became a member of the painter's guild of Florence. In 1476 he was denounced by the Night Watch, accused of immoral conduct, but was acquitted of this charge. In 1481 the monks of the Monastery of San Donato a Scopeto commissioned him to do the altar-piece of their church. This work, The Adoration of the Magi *(Uffizi), remained unfinished due to Leonardo's departure for Milan.*

As an envoy of Lorenzo the Magnificent, Leonardo arrived at the court of Ludovico il Moro to offer the lord of Milan a lyre, although Leonardo was the only one capable of playing it. Having completed his mission, Leonardo remained in Lombardy after having offered his services to Duke Ludovico il Moro, in a petition considered to be authentic although unsigned. The petition is now part of the Atlantic Codices. *In it are enumerated all the fields in which Leonardo could be used: military engineer, strategist, builder of arms, and in time of peace "composer" of buildings, hydraulic engineer, painter and sculptor. Leonardo was very active in Lombardy at the end of the fifteenth century. He occupied himself with the architecture of the cupola of the Duomo in Milan and of the Duomo and the Castle in Pavia. He painted the* Madonna of the Rocks *and the* Last Supper *for the Church of Santa Maria delle Grazie. He also set up the festivals of the court, designed the costumes, and directed the performances, including the famous "Feast of Paradise," presented at the Castle on January 13, 1490.*

In 1499 Ludovico il Moro fled Milan ahead of the oncoming French troops, while the Gascon bowmen of Louis XII used Leonardo's model for the equestrian statue of Francesco Sforza for target practice. Shortly afterward, Leonardo left Milan in spite of the evident good-will of the French authorities. He began his years of wandering. In Mantua, in the court of Isabella d'Este he sketched a portrait that he never completed. For a short time he stayed in Venice, where he was consultant for architectural matters from 1495 to 1499. In 1501, during a brief stay in Florence, he drew the cartoon of St. Anne for the altar-piece of the Saint Annunziata Church.

Between 1502 and 1503 he went to the Romagna region as a military engineer for Cesare Borgia. The death of Pope Alexander VI changed the fortunes of Duke Valentino, and Leonardo returned to Florence in 1503, remaining there until 1506. The Florentine Republic commissioned him to execute a large fresco of the battle of Anghiari for one of the walls of the Sala del Gran Consiglio in the Palazzo della Signoria facing a fresco by Michelangelo of the battle of Cascina. Leonardo experimented with a new technique and his fresco began to deteriorate almost immediately. In a matter of years it was completely destroyed. During these years he began the portrait of the Mona Lisa, *which he never gave to the person who commissioned the painting, later bringing it to France with a few other favorite works. In May 1506 he asked to be granted temporary leave from the Florentine Republic in order to return to Milan. He wanted to complete certain projects that he had left unfinished as the result of his hasty departure in 1499. Shortly before his flight, the Duke had given him a vineyard outside the Ludovica Gate as an acknowledgment of his services. This, along with the problem with the monks of San Francesco concerning his painting of the* Madonna of the Rocks, *made his stays in Florence shorter and rarer. In Milan, he once again came into contact with the French, and the governor of Milan, Charles d'Amboise, asked the Florentine Republic to extend Leonardo's leave, a request that was repeated a short time later by the King of France. Between 1507 and 1508 he was briefly in Florence to settle his father's estate with his brothers. He then spent many years in Milan having been given the title of "peintre et ingenieur ordinaire" and a fixed income. He devoted most of his time to scientific studies and to engineering projects such as the channeling of the course of the Adda river.*

The return of the Sforza family in 1512 forced Leonardo, now "compromised" because of his dealings with the French, to leave Milan once again. From 1513 to 1516 he was in Rome at the Palazzo Belvedere under the protection of Giuliano dei Medici, the brother of Pope Leo X. The presence in Rome of Michelangelo and Raphael, both much younger than he was, created a tense situation for Leonardo. Rome's competitive climate was much different from that of Milan, where he was the artistic leader of the city. With the death of his protector, Leonardo accepted the invitation of his French friends, and in 1516 he left Italy, never to return again. Accompanied by his faithful pupil, Melzi, he went to the castle of Cloux near Amboise. He took his best loved paintings with him, as well as the drawings and manuscripts which he later bequeathed to his favorite pupil.

Leonardo died on May 2, 1519, and was buried, according to his wishes, in the cloister of San Fiorentino in Amboise. His remains were dispersed during the ransack of the cloister by the Huguenots at the time of the religious wars.

". . . a painter can only be praised if he is universal." (Leonardo)

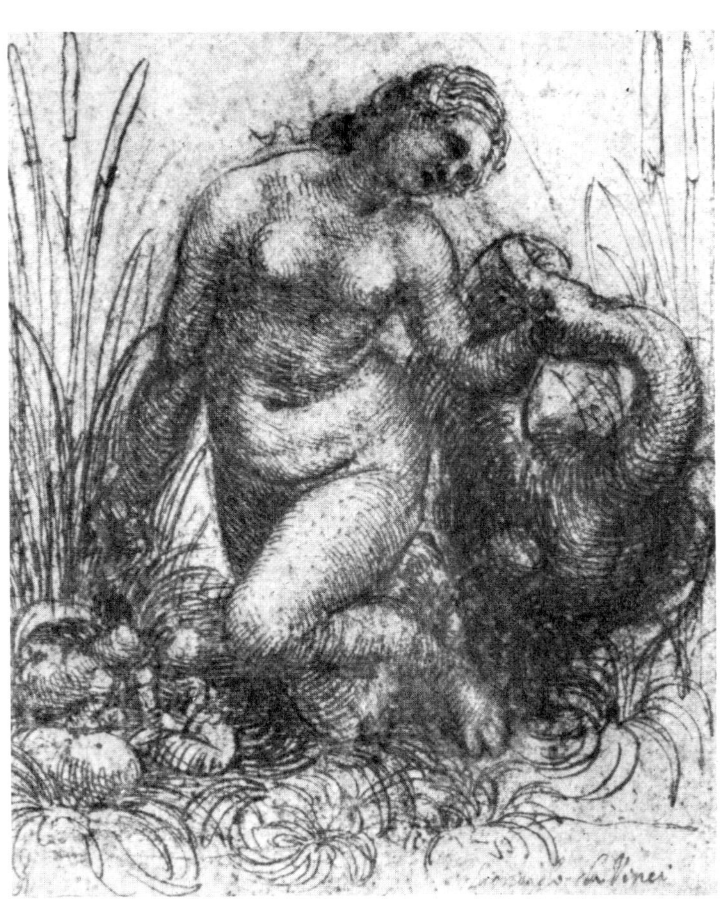

Leda, with the Swan—Rotterdam, Museum Boymans-Van Beunungen

The legend of Leonardo's universal genius was enhanced during the late nineteenth century when he was praised as the highest expression of Renaissance man, capable of solving all the world's problems—past, present and future. In reality, Leonardo was a man of many contradictions and uncertainties, with anxieties and problems that do not correspond to that image. These contradictions are reflected in his writings. They are reflected in his diverse thoughts, in his feverish search for the perfect form, and in his fragmentary notes where scientific observation is combined with philosophical reflections, where the anatomy of a human body is alternated with a violent polemic and a sententious aphorism, where the project of a war machine yields to the description of a flower. In his paintings, his dissatisfaction is manifested in his experiments with new techniques (often with disastrous results) and in works that remained incomplete or were not even begun. In contrast is the infinite, loving care that he applied to his favorite paintings.

Vasari exalted Leonardo as an artist who was "truly admirable and celestial," a tribute that this historian from Arezzo granted to all the "divine" masters of the Italian cinquecento. He cautiously added that "Leonardo . . . would have greatly profited, if he was not of such varied and unstable humor. For he began to learn many things, and once begun, he would abandon them."

The demystification of the personality of Leonardo, which began with the famed lecture by Croce in 1906 on the limits of Leonardo as a philosopher and has continued in various degrees to our day, touches almost all aspects of the master's personality. It's intention is to "see Leonardo within the framework of his epoch, in his effective historical dimension, in his real human dimension free of any myth which is perhaps the best manner to honor a man who had a sense of measure that I can define as chaste." So wrote Garin in 1952, in celebration of the fifth centenary of Leonardo's birth, in a perspicacious examination of late fifteenth century Florentine culture.

Leonardo is the most significant exponent of the Florentine culture of the day. The men of his time were open to every field of interest, conscious of their strength and of their intelligence, but were at the same time caught up in the agitation of a world in change. Another century was to pass before the arrival of Galileo's new science or the pictorial revolution of Caravaggio.

Falling back on the principle that one must begin with the experience of natural phenomena to be a good painter, "that the painter will not achieve excellent results if he chooses as a model the paintings of others," Leonardo positioned himself as an equal to Giotto and Masaccio. He assumed the same weight they had in the artistic events of their epoch, but in contrast to them, he did not go beyond his times, nor could he. He was more attracted to criticism than to innovation, more interested in speculation than in practical results, and tended to doubt rather than affirm an idea.

He entered Verrocchio's crowded workshop when he was seventeen, collaborating with the master and the other disciples. On the solid framework of Verrocchio's compositions, on the master's emaciated and jutting figures he began to exercise the subtleties of his brushwork. "Oh, you anatomical painter, be careful lest your having too much knowledge of the bones, the sinews, and the muscles will make you become a stiff painter," wrote Leonardo at a later date. He perhaps recalled the atmosphere of Verrocchio's workshop, with the strident and cruel sign of the line, and the continual anatomical researches developed by Florentine sculpture and painting. Leonardo applied a softer skin, a lighter chiaroscuro, to the crude anatomies of his master, but without abandoning the Florentine tradition of beautiful drawing and chiaroscuro. There emerges from this period the *Madonna* in Sheffield where the airy, romantically crumbling architecture and the tender face of the Virgin seem worthy of the work of the young student. From the same period we see the *Madonna di Piazza* in the Duomo of Pistoia; Verrocchio was commissioned to do it but evidently gave it to the mediocre Lorenzo di Credi. In that work the altarpiece, now at the Louvre, repeats on a smaller scale and with more essential forms the famous *Annunciation* (Uffizi). The most famous work done in collaboration with Verrocchio is the *Baptism of Christ* (Uffizi). Here Leonardo made the beautiful blond and languid angel on the left side of the painting as well as part of the landscape above the heads of the angels where the waters and the mountains vibrate and blend with the subtle veil of the atmosphere. Even Leonardo's first independent works, the Madonnas, now in Munich and Leningrad and the *Annunciation,* so similar to the bronzed sarcophagus of Giovanni and Piero de Medici, follow the Florentine line. In the wings of the angel one can see the results of his studies of the flight of birds. "The great bird shall take flight and will fill the world with his fame," wrote Leonardo in his *Codex of the Flight of Birds.* These words, besides being an illuminating prophecy, express his desire to understand the mechanism of the wing, the secret that in his dreams could render human flight possible.

From this period is the portrait of the so-called *Ginevra Benci* (Vaduz, Lichtenstein Gallery), with its unflinching physiological research that goes from the Flemish style to the Florentine portrait style of the period. Leonardo implies with the painting of this face something hidden and veiled that would reach its zenith in the painting of the *Mona Lisa.* "Imagine the faces of men and women on a street at dusk, when the weather is bad, how much grace and sweetness one can see in them . . . this is the perfect atmosphere." Leonardo's subtle transition in tone is not, however, a natural effect, due to the atmosphere. It is not the result of the tradition of Tuscan culture of the end of the fifteenth century, when drawing and chiaroscuro were the two principal expressive tenets. "Do not try to imitate the transparent leaves in the light of sun, for it only leads to confusion," he warned in his *Treatise on Painting.* He warned against purely "impressionistic" effects, and he plunged his figures into an almost misty, hazy light. Leonardo insists, in his manuscripts, in pointing out the effects of light and shadow, defining shadow as "primitive," "derivative," "repercussive," "simple," but then tells us that "large and strong illumination will render the parts of the bodies very pleasing." It is the "universal light," so liked by the painters of the cinquecento, that envelops the figures and the landscapes in an immobile timeless atmosphere.

The *Adoration of the Magi* for the Church of San Donato a Scopeto was the first large work undertaken by Leonardo when he

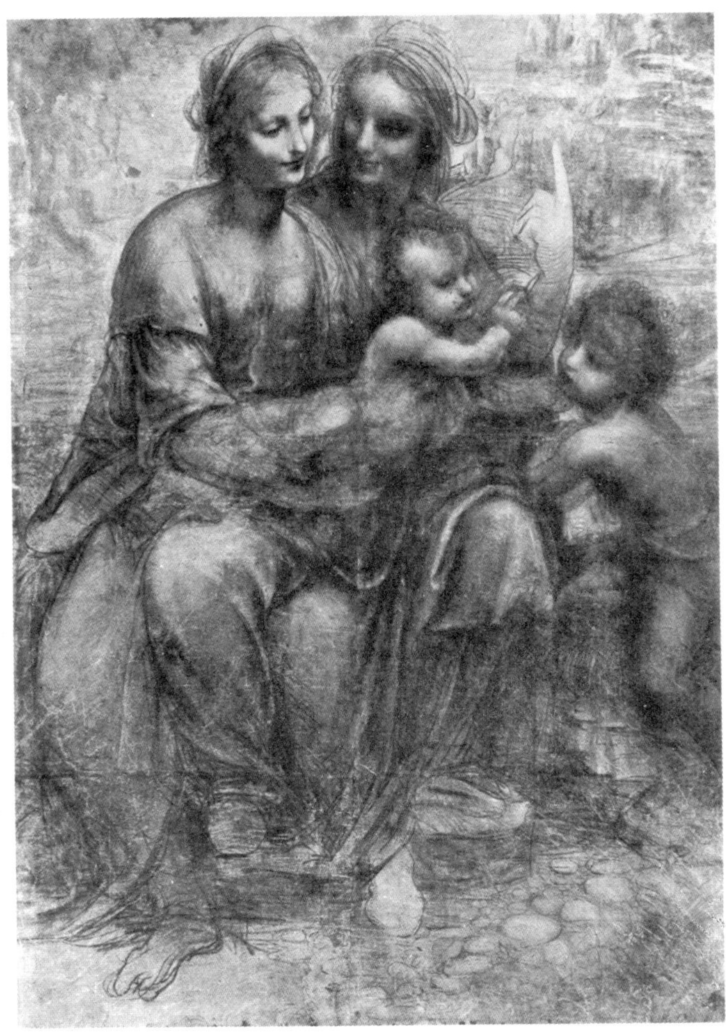

Cartoon for St. Anne with the Madonna and Child—London, Royal Academy of Arts.

was almost thirty years old. Several years before, in 1478, he had been commissioned to do an altar-piece for the chapel of San Bernardo in the Palazzo della Signoria. Leonardo delayed, and the commission went to the young painter Filippino Lippi. This became the *Altar of the Eight of Pratica* of 1485, now in the Uffizi. *The Adoration* has perhaps the boldest composition of all of Leonardo's works, even when compared to his later paintings such as the *Madonna of the Rocks* with its pyramidal structure, or the *Last Supper* with its rigorous division in threes. As Longhi said of the *Adoration,* it has a "multidirectional and rapid circulation" of the figures that surround the Holy Family, from which emanates a supernatural light that reflects on the onlookers in varied degrees and intensity.

"The working out of the composition must be complete, the delineation of the parts of the body must remain incomplete; the painter must remain satisfied with the tracings of these parts, and so, at a later date, at his ease, and if he finds pleasure, he may complete the work." This sentence helps us to understand a work such as the *Adoration:* the "working out of the composition" of the subject entrusted to his unerring hand, as in the extraordinary section of the battle of the horsemen in the background of the painting, animated by the highlighting of white lead. This must have been more satisfying for Leonardo than the finished drawings, which were either rapid and bold or timorous and subtle. The initial ideas for his paintings, the illustrations and comments to his scientific notes, were often subtle poetical works rather than impassive scientific documents. This can be seen in his drawings of flowers and animals, and even, at times, in his crudest anatomical studies, or in his drawings of the stratification of the terrestrial crust, in his "deluges," in the "tornados" of water and wind.

Leonardo prepared for the fresco of the *Last Supper* for the refectory of the Church of Santa Maria delle Grazie in Milan with many studies and detailed annotations in which he recorded gestures, faces and expressions. Choosing the moment when Christ announced to the apostles the coming betrayal, Leonardo used expressions of anxiety and dramatic gestures as well as a psy-

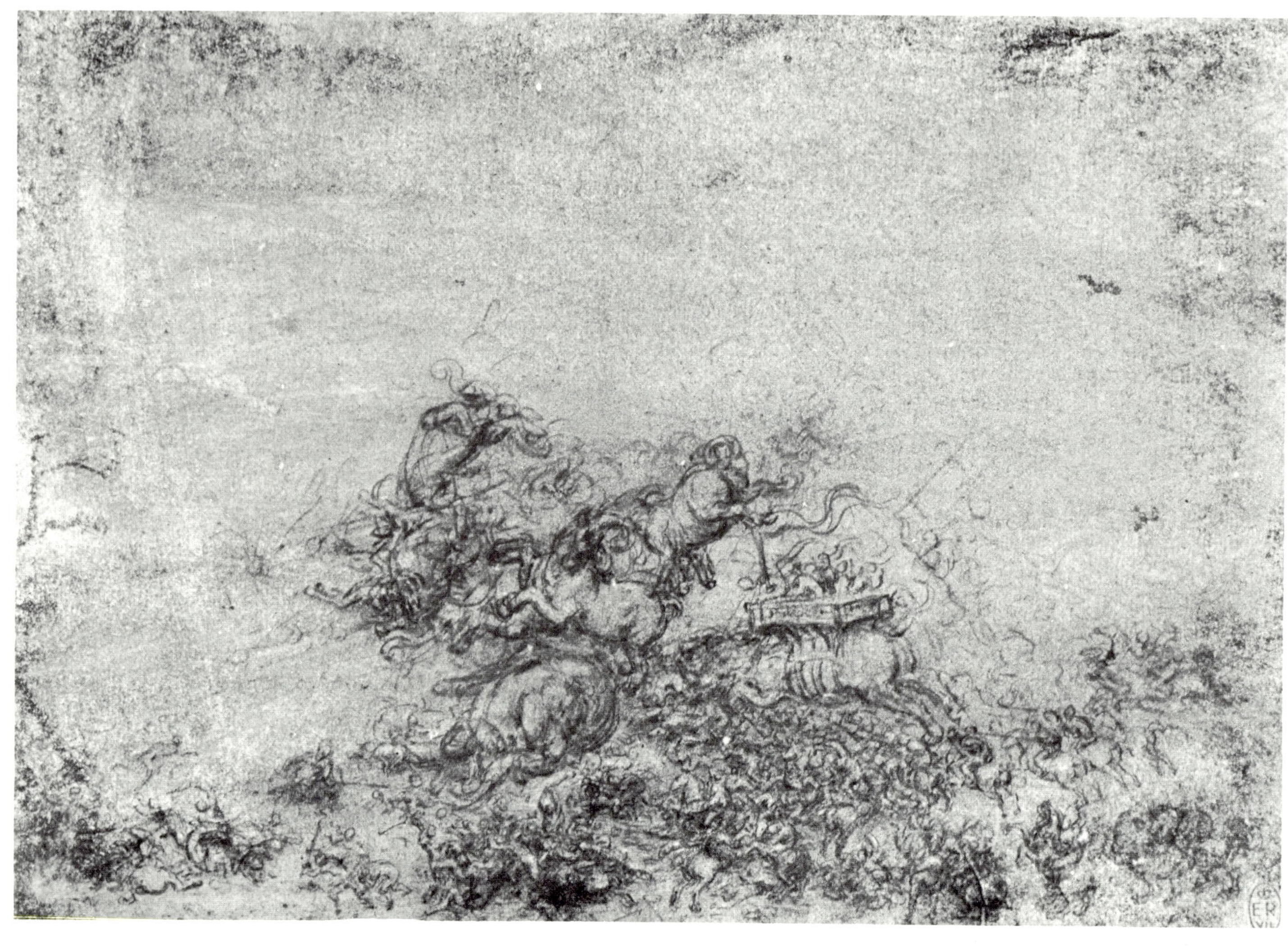

Study of animals and knights fighting—Windsor, Royal Library. (Kindly granted by Her Majesty Queen Elisabeth II, copyright reserved)

chological study of all the characters. This swept aside the rigid symmetrical disposition of the Tuscan Last Suppers of the quattrocento, even though the composition was based on Florentine rigor of arranging the figures in groups of three.

In Milan, Leonardo painted the signed version of the *Madonna of the Rocks,* where everything—rocks and flowers, human figures and shrubs—is pervaded with the same vitality: an "animism" that ranges from the skin of the bodies to the solidity of the rocks, from the petal of a flower to the shimmering of the water. In a fragment of the *Leicester Codex,* Leonardo affirms that the earth has a "vegetative soul." He found subtle parallels between living structures and the composition of the earth: mountains are the bones of this immense organism; the tufa the cartilages; the veins of water the blood; the ebb and flow of the sea the breath of respiration; the "infused fire of the earth: the volcanos the abode of the vegetative soul of the world," the sea, conceived in the Ptolemaic manner as the immense river that encircles the world, "the sea of blood that surrounds the heart."

With a certain sense of coyness, Leonardo speaks of himself in his writings as "not being a man of letters," though he had a vast and up-to-date cultural background, even if fragmentary and in certain areas confused. He was proud of the fact that when confronted with the trumpets and the "repeaters" he was unable "to comment on the ones high up," that is, to comment on the sacred texts, the sources of ancient wisdom. He had instead learned everything from experience, this master of masters. But in his desire to know everything about a subject, to discover the inner essence of men and plants, flowers and animals, he did not achieve a greater awareness or grasp of reality than Masaccio achieved seventy years earlier in his depiction of barren hills. He created a fantastic and unreal world, an antelitteram romanticism. He was fascinated by changeable aspects of the universe, the fleeting essence of things. "The water that one touches is the last of that which has passed and the first of that which is to come, and so is the present instant," is a reflection found in Leonardo's *Codex Trivulziano,* which paraphrased an ancient maxim of Heraclitus. "Oh, time, consumer of things . . ." is another of his evocations, and he invites us to "look at the light and observe its beauty. Close your eyes for an instant and look at it again. What you saw no longer exists, and that which it was is no longer there." These thoughts can best explain one of his most famous paintings, the *Mona Lisa,* which has had an almost morbid fascination for critics and for the public (see Pater's writings). The expression of the face, the famous smile, is elusive and ephemeral as the impalpable essence of the flaking rocks that reflect in the green-blue waters.

In Florence, while he endlessly caressed the face of the *Mona Lisa* with his brush, the Republic commissioned him to paint the battle of Anghiari, an episode of the war between Florence and the Visconti. This was painted on one of the walls of the Sala del Gran Consiglio in the Palazzo Vecchio, now the Salone of the Cinquecento, as a companion piece of Michelangelo's episode of the war with Pisa, the battle of Cascina, scheduled to be painted on the opposite wall. As a result of those unsuccessful technical experiments of Leonardo, the *Battle of Anghiari,* a "vast mixture of colors" that were not rapidly absorbed into the wall, deteriorated quickly and faded completely after just a few years. On the opposite wall, what was to have been Michelangelo's fresco of the battle of Cascina was never done. The large cartoon, cut into pieces, was lost in the confusion that followed the return of the Medici to Florence in 1512. Leonardo's famous work can be reconstructed only through the numerous copies that were made, like the one by Rubens, executed in the baroque style, or from the many drawings and notes with which Leonardo documented the various phases of the battle, and from the extensive discussions in a passage of the *Atlantic Codex* on "the means of representing a battle." In contrast to the stylized nudes that Michelangelo had represented in his painting, choosing the moment when the Florentines were bathing in the Arno and surprised by the Pisans, Leonardo portrayed the furious vortex of men and horses during the most intense moment of the battle. Vasari commented that "this battle expresses the complete rage, the contempt and the revenge of both men and horses, two of which are interlocked with their forelegs. They fight with their teeth, no less fiercely than their riders who are struggling for the standard."

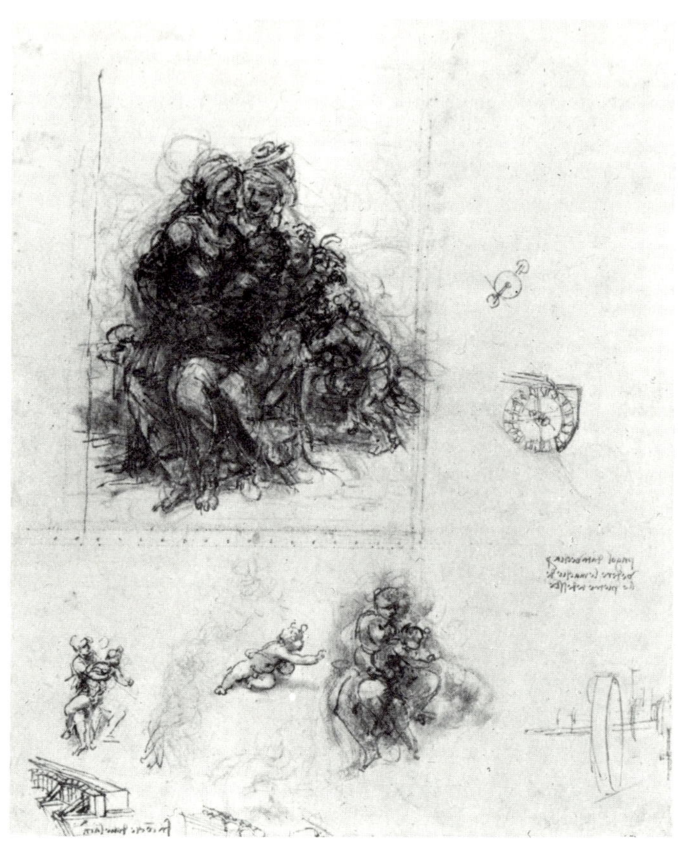

Study of the Madonna with St. Anne, St. Anne, and mechanical drawings—London, British Museum (By courtesy of the Administrators of the British Museum).

When Leonardo returned to Milan he almost abandoned painting completely. "Another among the greatest painters in the world holds in contempt that art which is so rare," Baldassar Castiglione wrote with regret and with a touch of irony in his *The Courtier,* evidently alluding to Leonardo. "He has decided to learn philosophy of which he has strange concepts and new illusions that he, in all of his writings, is not able to describe." It was in this period that Leonardo made the painting based on the cartoon of *St. Anne,* which a decade before had been admired by the people of Florence. The painting itself, a bit undertone and nebulous, due in part to the evident work of his students, is truly inferior to the subtleness of the preparatory drawings for the cartoon, which is perhaps the first version of the famous altarpiece. During these years the De Predis brothers, under the guidance of the master, completed the copy of the *Madonna of the Rocks,* begun during the last years of the fifteenth century for the Chapel of the Concezione in San Francesco Grande in Milan and now in the National Gallery in London.

It was perhaps during his brief stay in Rome that Leonardo made the ambiguous and delicate *St. John the Baptist* that he took with him to France. A few other works, now lost, are from these last years: a *Judith,* a *Madonna and Child* painted in Rome for Baldassarre Turini, datary of Pope Leon X, and the famous *Leda* which Leonardo seemed to have made in Rome for his protector Giuliano dei Medici, of which there are numerous variations and interpretations by painters of the epoch. It was in France that Leonardo finally attained the position of privilege that he always wanted. Adapting himself to the competitive artistic circles of Florence and Rome had been difficult. He had always preferred Milan, where he could dedicate himself to his favorite studies and where he was the unchallenged master, surrounded, in the eyes of his world, by a halo of mystery.

According to Leonardo, painting is "the principal intellectual discourse." In contrast, a sculptor has to use a mechanical physical force "in maneuvering the mallet and the chisel," and is always covered with dust and sweat, whereas the painter appears as the ideal person for the taste and the tendencies of the master. "In his ease the painter sits in front of his work, well dressed, and moves the very light brush with which he applies his colors, and wears garments that are pleasing to him, and his dwelling is replete with the most varied paintings and is clean, and he is often accompanied by music and readings of various and beautiful works, which, without the din of the mallet or of other various sounds, are pleasing to be heard." (*Urbinate Codex,* c. 36).

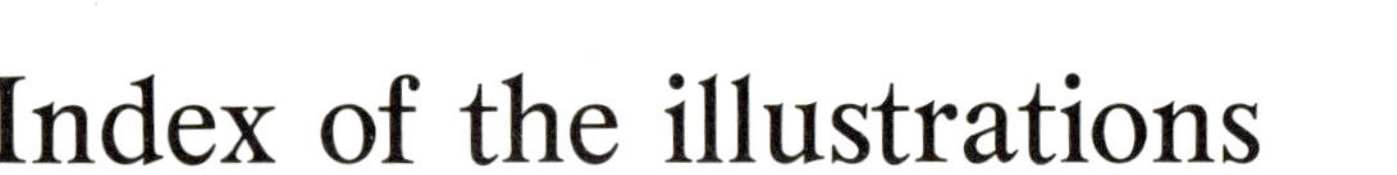

Index of the illustrations

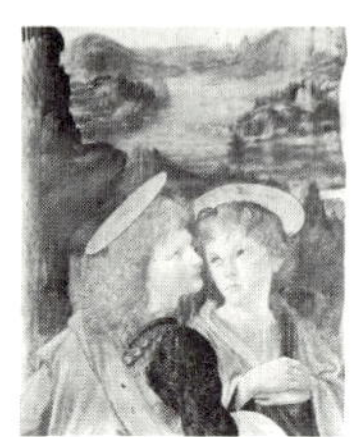

I - Angels and landscape of the Baptism of Christ, by Verrocchio - Florence, Galleria degli Uffizi - *Verrocchio was commissioned for the painting in the 8th decade of the 15th century. Leonardo collaborated in the execution of the work by painting the angel on the left—which is delicate and nuanced when compared to the sharp and well defined drawing of the angel next to it—as well as the landscape in the background.*

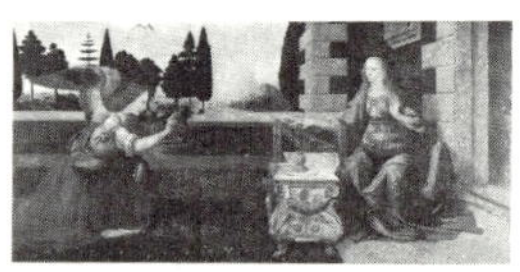

II-III - Annunciation - Florence, Galleria degli Uffizi - *It was painted for the convent of San Bartolomeo di Monteoliveto between 1475 and 1478. In contrast to the Virgin enclosed within the stone niche, the angel appears within the space of the broad landscape delineated by the somber trees. The axis of the composition is the luminous opening of the distant landscape.*

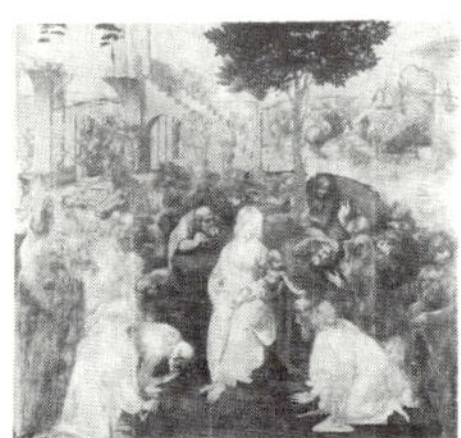

IV - Adoration of the Magi - Florence, Galleria degli Uffizi - *Commissioned by the monks of San Donato in Scopeto, it was left unfinished when Leonardo went to Milan. On the prepared brown background one can see the main chromatic areas of the painting: deep masses of shadow, figures that emerge due to the few rapid touches of white lead.*

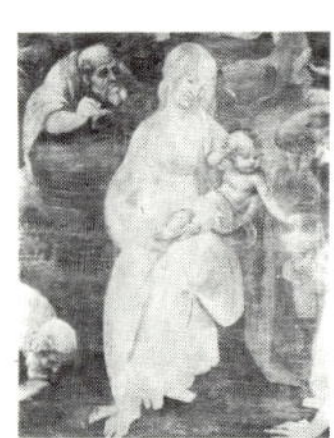

V - Adoration of the Magi - (detail of the central part of the painting) - Florence, Galleria degli Uffizi - *With this painting Leonardo renewed the compositional tradition of the 15th century with the rhythm and balance that he had used in his* Annunciation. *The Virgin and Child are now in the center of a vortex of figures that are infused, in various degrees, by the light emanating from the sacred group.*

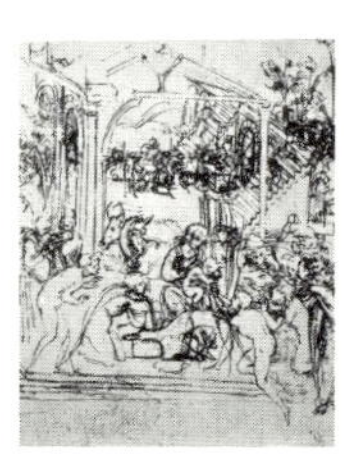

VI - Preparatory drawing for the Adoration of the Magi - Paris, Musée du Louvre - *Drawing, as can be read in Leonardo's* Treatise on Painting, *had great significance for him. It was much more than making a simple sketch that was to be perfected in the painting. In his drawings Leonardo studied the various solutions from which he would choose the most adequate to transfer to the canvas.*

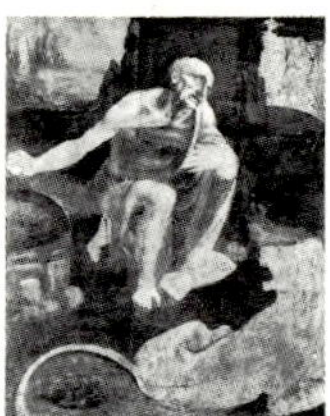

VII - St. Jerome - Rome, Vatican Museum - *This is another of Leonardo's unfinished works, one that he began a short time before 1482. It was found in a junk shop in Rome in 1820 by Cardinal Fesch. The bold foreshortening of the face with its deep lines reveals Leonardo's passionate anatomical studies that are here transcribed with a sure and rapid hand.*

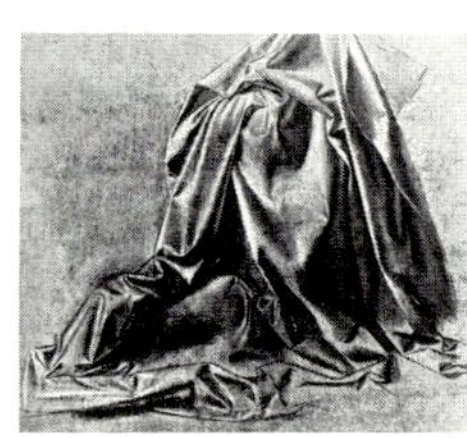

VIII - Study of drapery - Paris, Musée du Louvre - *In his notebooks, Leonardo has left us a testimony of some of his conceptions on technique and esthetics. When writing on drapery he says that the drape must reveal the figure of the wearer, as well as the pose of the subject. He advises avoiding "the confusion of too many folds."*

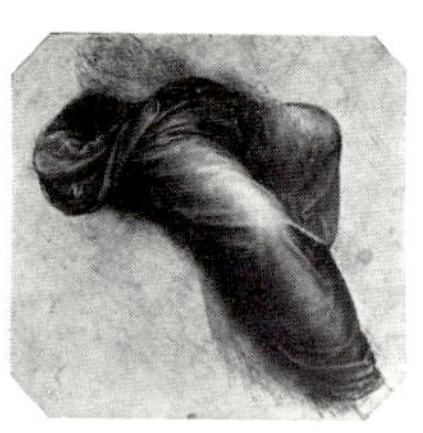

IX - Study for the drapes of the Virgin with St. Anne - Paris, Musée du Louvre - *Leonardo made many drawings for the group of the Virgin with St. Anne. Critics agree in attributing this drawing to a later period, around 1510, because of the complex technique used by the artist: black pencil with watercolor and white lead.*

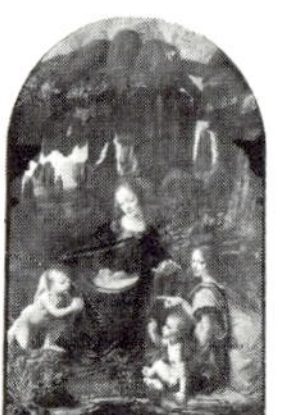

X - The Virgin of the Rocks - Paris, Musée du Louvre - *A later version done by De Predis, that is now at the National Gallery in London, is the painting which is mentioned in the contract of 1483 and which concerned the lengthy dispute between the brotherhood and the painter over the delay in the consignment of the painting. The painting in the Louvre is a signed version made during Leonardo's first years in Milan.*

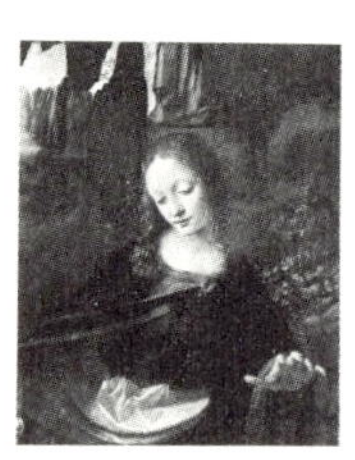

XI - The Virgin of the Rocks - (detail of the landscape) - Paris, Musée du Louvre - *It is in these details of the landscape, replete with subtle and mysterious resonances, that one can feel the implications of Leonardo's painting: in the magical rocks in the background one can recognize the same troubled spiritual life that defines the Virgin's highly sensitive face.*

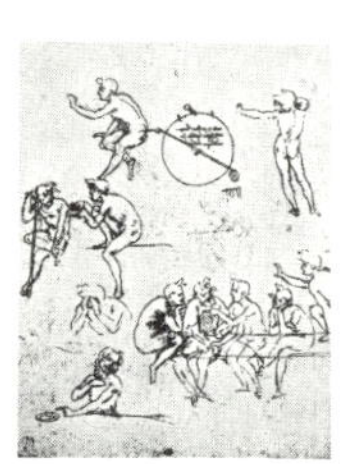

XII - Study of figures and composition for the Last Supper - Paris, Musée du Louvre - *This is one of the drawings that Leonardo made for the composition of the* Last Supper. *This study depicts some of the positions of the Apostles and Christ. We know from other drawings that he thought of other iconographic solutions, as in the drawing now found at Windsor that represents the moment of the Eucharist.*

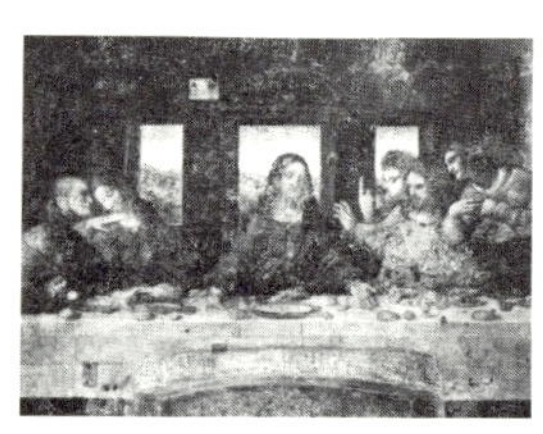

XIII - Last Supper - (detail) - Milan, Refectory of S. Maria delle Grazie - *This work represents the height of Leonardo's expressive power using every element in its specific pictorial vocabulary, as with the supernatural figure of Christ surrounded by the Apostles, each one of whom expresses, according to his age and his character, either terror, or surprise, or sorrow.*

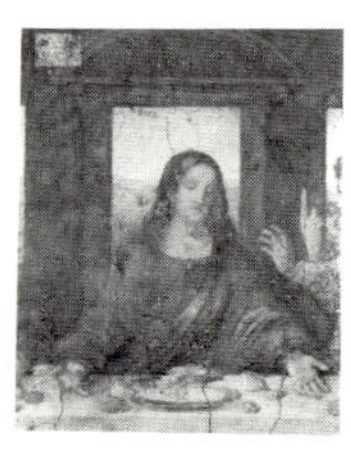

XIV - Last Supper - (detail of Christ) - Milan, Refectory of S. Maria delle Grazie - *According to Vasari Leonardo did not "perfect" the head of Christ as he could find no model that could express "that beauty and celestial grace." The* Last Supper *has recently been restored by M. Pelliccioli, who has brought to light Leonardo's brushstrokes, even though they are in a bad state of preservation.*

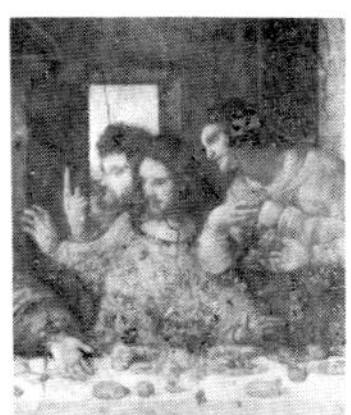

XV - Last Supper - (detail) - Milan, Refectory of S. Maria delle Grazie - *The fresco was made between 1495 and 1497; a few years later it began to deteriorate rapidly, due to Leonardo's unusual technique and to the humidity in the wall. Restorations that were made over the centuries in the hope of saving this precious work have actually hastened its deterioration.*

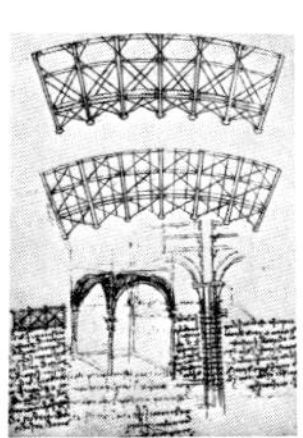

XVI - Drawings of armatures and scaffolding for festivals - Paris, Institut de France, Manuscript B, fol. 28 verso - *During his stay in Milan, Leonardo, the genius of mechanics, occupied himself with the problems of theater and festival decoration. The most exacting of these works was for the organization of the wedding reception of Ludovico il Moro and Beatrice d'Este.*

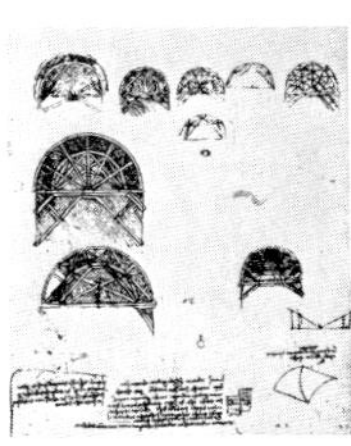

XVII - Drawing of studies for various types of centerings - Atlantic Codex, fol. 200, recto - a - *That Leonardo wanted to write an architectural treatise can be deduced from the quantity of notes (never put together), sketches, and drawings that he left. The numerous annotations that are addressed directly to the reader clearly demonstrate his intention to explain as well as illustrate.*

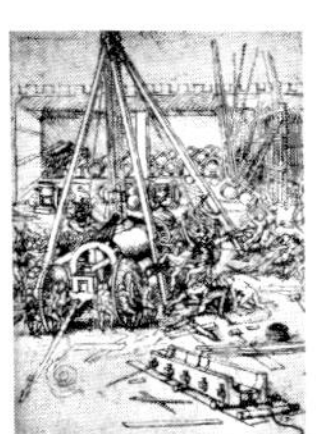

XVIII - Drawing of a cannon foundry - London, Royal Coll. of Windsor, no. 12647 - *As the ducal engineer of the Sforza and chief engineer for Duke Valentino, Leonardo had the chance to study, design, and elaborate new methods for the construction of offensive and defensive weapons whose brilliant originality was only understood and appreciated centuries later.*

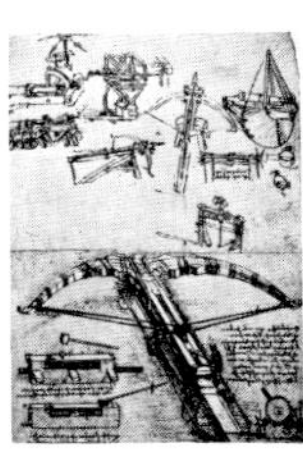

XIX - Drawing of a large crossbow with inclined wheel and other crossbows - Atlantic Codex, fol. 53, verso -a-b - *Leonardo studied innumerable types of throwing weapons, both mobile and fixed, of enormous proportions which no one until then had conceived. He left detailed descriptions of their practical use.*

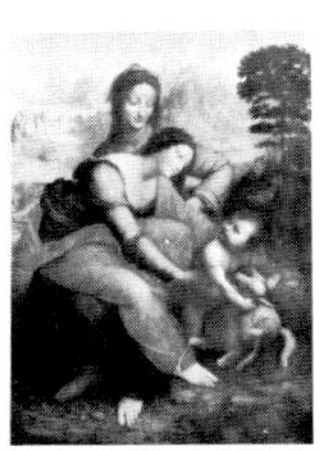

XX - The Virgin and Child with St. Anne - Paris, Musée du Louvre - *Leonardo was commissioned to do this work at the beginning of the 16th century for the church Sts. Annunziata in Florence. In 1501, the cartoon for the work was exhibited to the public, and it was enthusiastically received. The cartoon at the Royal Academy in London is another version of this famous composition.*

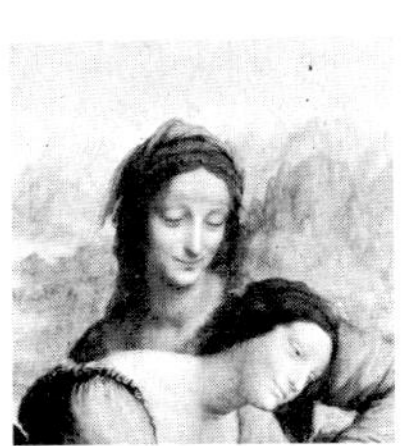

XXI - The Virgin and Child with St. Anne - (detail) - Paris, Musée du Louvre - *It was only around 1510, and with the help of his students, that Leonardo made the painting based on the cartoon, but it was never sent to Florence, for he brought it with him to France. It returned to Italy with Melzi, but in 1630 it was purchased by Richelieu and so returned permanently to France.*

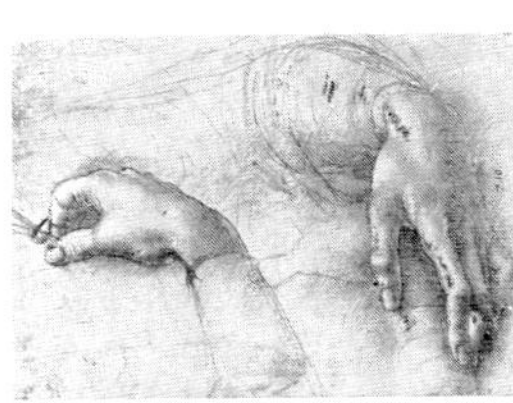

XXII - Study of woman's hands and small caricature sketches of virile heads - London, Royal Coll. of Windsor, no. 12558 - *Various hypotheses have been proposed on the relationship between the study of the hands and some of Leonardo's paintings; but there is no proof that they were used in the portrait of* Ginevra Benci, *or in the painting of the* Mona Lisa, *executed many years before.*

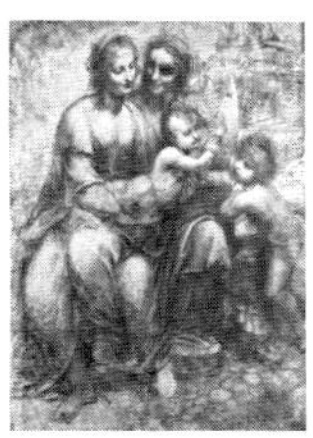

XXIII - Virgin with St. Anne, the Child and St. John - London, National Gallery - *This iconographic theme was often treated by Leonardo, in drawings such as this cartoon, as well as in the painting in the Louvre. Though it is difficult to give a precise date to them, it is quite probable that this cartoon is of 1501.*

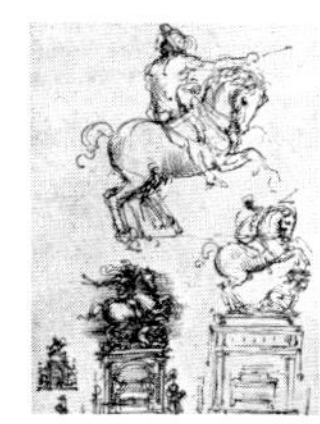

XXIV - Study for the equestrian monument of Field-marshal Trivulzio - London, Royal Coll. of Windsor, no. 12355 - *It is most likely that the idea of this monument—never executed—goes back to the period immediately following the defeat of the Sforza house in Milan by the troops of the king of France under the leadership of the Milanese commander Trivulzio.*

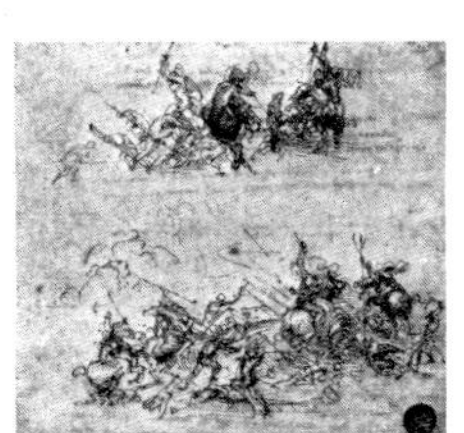

XXV - Sketches for the battle of Anghiari - Venice, Academy - *The sketches in this series seem to refer to the most important part of the famous cartoon (now lost) on the culminating phase of the action: the ultimate struggle for the conquest of the standard. Other studies on the battle of Anghiari are found in the Royal Collection of Windsor.*

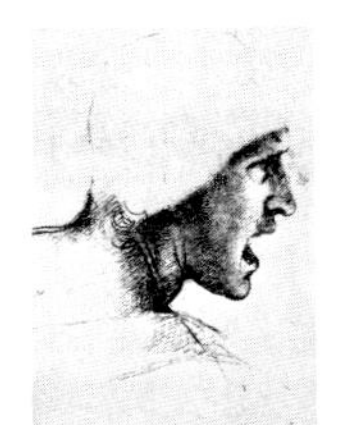

XXVI - Study for the head of a soldier for the battle of Anghiari - Budapest, National Museum of Fine Arts - *This is one of the many sketches that reveal how Leonardo, especially in working out complex paintings with several perspectives and the grouping of numerous subjects, spent a great deal of time in the minute study of anatomy and kinetics. This explains the great number of drawings and cartoons that refer to the same theme.*

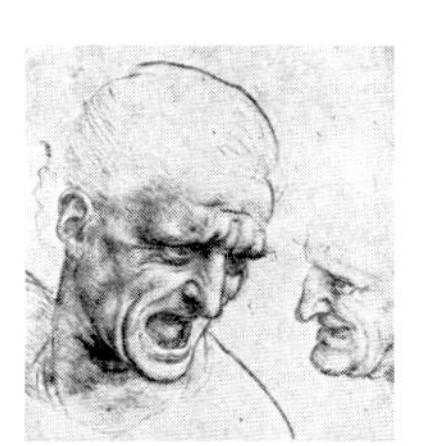

XXVII - Study of two soldier's heads for the battle of Anghiari - Budapest, National Museum of Fine Arts - *We know from a description by Vasari, who admired Leonardo's painting in the Sala del Gran Consiglio in the Palazzo Vecchio, that this study refers to the central group of horsemen who fought to control the standard.*

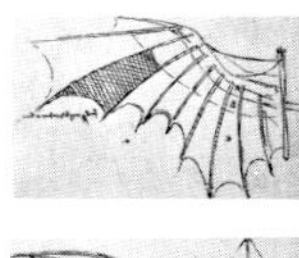

XXVIII - Project of a wing with nerves partly covered with taffeta and a machine with a crank to make the wings beat - Atlantic Codex, fol. 313 recto - a - *Leonardo became interested in mechanical flight during his stay in Milan and continued his studies at Fiesole. There, as a result of his observations of the wings of birds, he conceived of fascinating devices that were extremely precise and integrated human muscle power.*

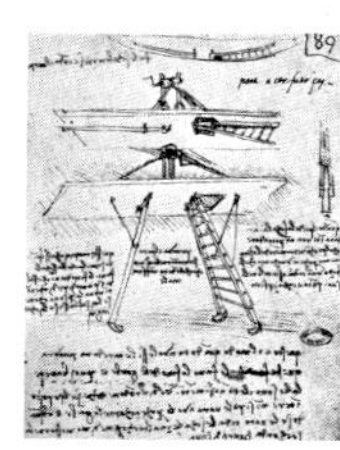

XXIX - Flying device - Paris, Institut de France, Manuscript D, fol. 89 recto - *Having realized the impossibility of flight based solely on muscular power Leonardo built mechanical devices that were often very elaborate, as is the one represented in this drawing, and foresaw that a man in an erect position would be able to maintain a constant equilibrium while manipulating four wings and two pedals.*

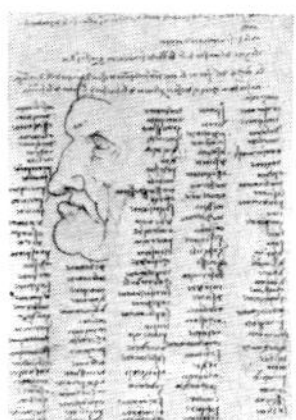

XXX - Series of words with a caricatured profile - Trivulziano Codex, plate 54, fol. 30 recto - *A great number of Leonardo's notes deal with the study of grammar. Many critics have maintained that they had a didactic purpose, while more recent studies have found in these documents, "the efforts of the founder of Italian scientific prose" to define certain terms (E. Solmi).*

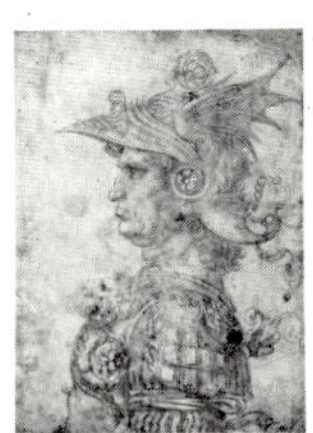

XXXI - The Condottiere - London, British Museum - *This drawing, done in silverpoint, is one of the innumerable testimonies of the range of interests that occupied Leonardo; or rather, it represents the infinite means that he used in his passion for research with a mind that knew no limits: from the arts to mechanics, from anatomy to botany, as well as all the other scientific fields.*

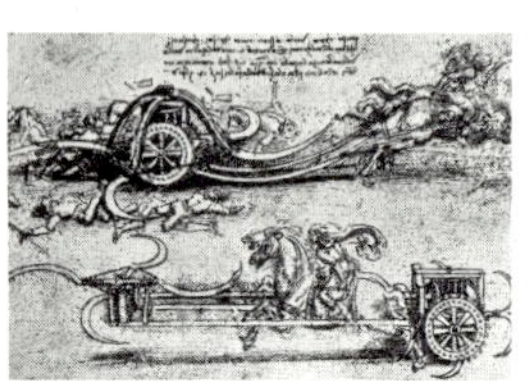

XXXII - Drawing of a scythed vehicle - Turin, Biblioteca Reale - *In the field of military technology Leonardo anticipated many inventions and solutions that were only understood and applied centuries later. The first studies of this type were dedicated to the offensive and defensive techniques for the battlefield. This drawing of a scythed vehicle is a very original example of the use for which it was intended.*

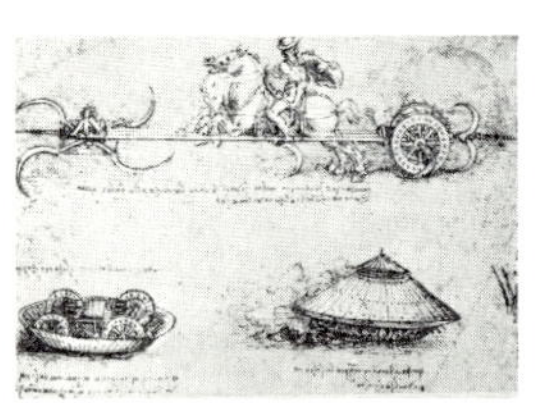

XXXIII - Drawing of a scythed vehicle and a covered armored car - London, British Museum - *The ingenious elaboration of various war machines, like this surprising covered car, the ancestor of the modern tank, is followed by Leonardo's description of its function and tactical use. Disruptive action by the vehicle, before the infantry moves in is a tactic that has remained unchanged to our day.*

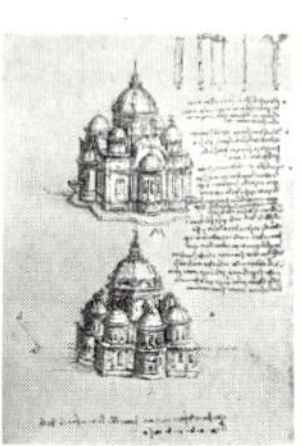

XXXIV - Drawings of domed churches with the central-plan and a study of the relationship of proportions - Ms. B, fol. 17 verso - *Leonardo dealt at length with architectural themes, even if his studies almost always remained theoretical, and he rarely dealt with concrete problems. These sketches show how he envisaged the equilibrium and harmony of proportions that characterized Italian Renaissance architecture.*

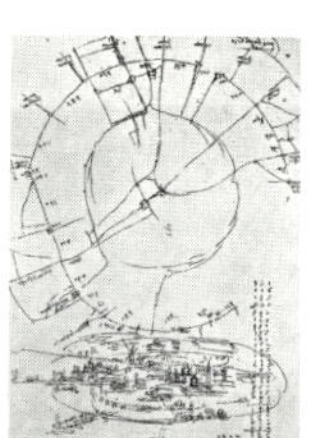

XXXV - Drawing of the plan and a panoramic perspective of the city of Milan - Atlantic Codex - *Leonardo's architectural concepts were based on the intention of harmonizing the surroundings with man's needs. The oldest drawings go back to the first period in Milan during which Leonardo worked out the scheme of a decentralized urban "chessboard" that spread out into the surrounding countryside.*

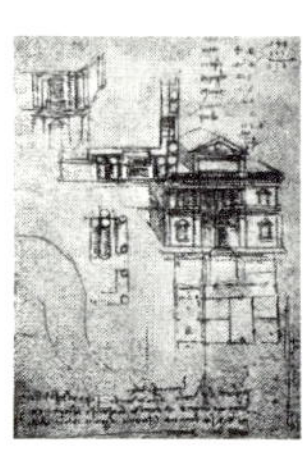

XXXVI - Perspective drawing, plan and various elements of a lordly villa - Turin, Biblioteca Reale, Ms. of the Codex of the Flight of Birds - *The architectural theme is developed by Leonardo not only from the artistic point of view, but from the scientific view as well. His projects become studies of the materials, a research in perspective and in the equilibrium of the structure itself.*

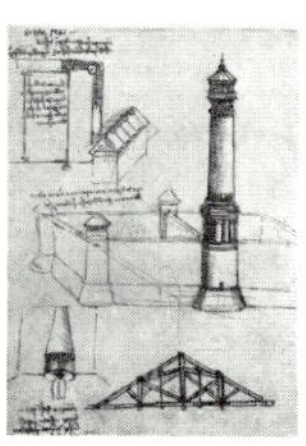

XXXVII - Architectural drawings and a project for a tower - Paris, Institut de France, Ms. B, fol. 23 verso - *The most interesting aspect of Leonardo's architectural studies is in the research for the modernization of the traditional forms and techniques. He introduced more rational criteria for the solution of the problems of defense as well as in investigating the problems of the interplay between independent elements.*

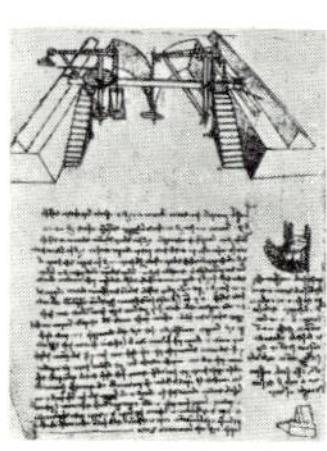

XXXVIII - Drawing for hoisting machines for the transportation of excavated materials from a canal under construction - Atlantic Codex, fol. 363 verso - b - *The creation and the rational use of canals had interested Leonardo from the point of view of urban planning, as a means of transportation, and as a technical problem of hydraulics; the exploitation of the velocity and the flow of the water.*

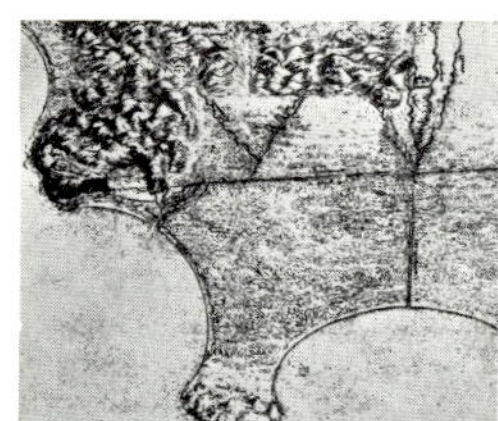

XXXIX - Drawing for the project of the land reclamation of the Pontine swamps - London, Royal Coll. of Windsor, no. 12684 - *During Leonardo's stay at Rome he developed this ambitious project whose realization was greatly encouraged by Pope Leo X. Leonardo planned one large canal that was to run parallel to the Via Appia, and whose capacity was great enough to drain and carry away the whole of the stagnant mass of the swamp.*

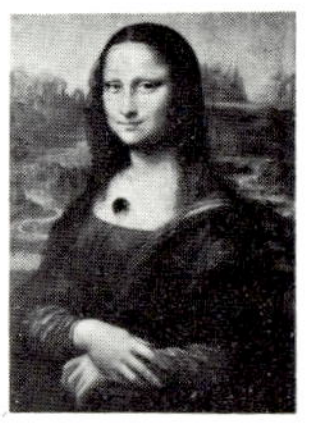

XL-XLI - Mona Lisa - Paris, Musée du Louvre - *This painting, one of the most famous in the world, is traditionally identified as the portrait of Monna Lisa del Giocondo that was mentioned by Vasari, and begun in Florence around the year 1503. Leonardo never consigned the work, for he brought it to France among his most cherished possessions.*

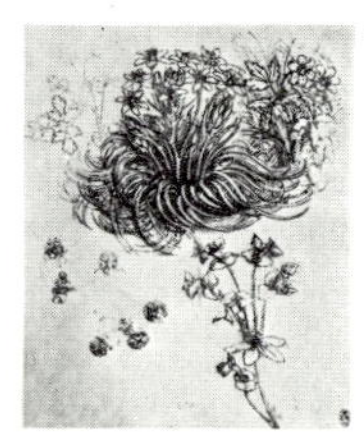

XLII - Drawing of Ornithogalum Umbellatum (above) and of a Euphorbia (below) - London, Royal Coll. of Windsor, no. 12424 - *From the observation of nature, Leonardo became fascinated by the world of plants to the point of searching for the general laws of the forms and the development of plants. He was the first person to have scientifically established the fundamental principles of botany.*

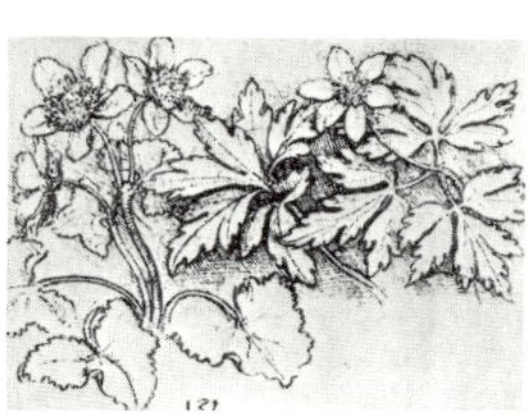

XLIII - Drawing of a Nemrosa anemone - London, Royal Coll. of Windsor, no. 12423 - *Leonardo's interest in botany goes back to his youth. In his 20s he had already made a large number of drawings of plants, replete with the most minute details and extremely precise. Later on he depicted the individual organs of every plant, thereby intuiting the affinities among certain species.*

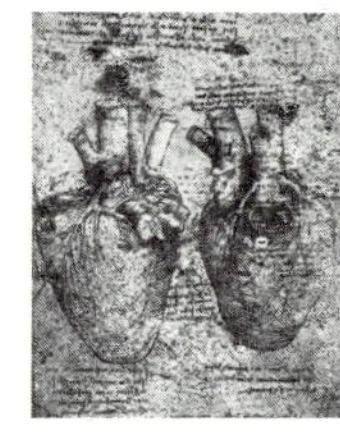

XLIV - Drawing of the heart and its blood vessels - Milan, Ambrosiana - Anatomical notebooks, Vol. II, fol. 3 verso - *Leonardo was the first in the history of anatomical drawings to represent the heart from different perspectives and in its most minute details. The heart was the principal object of his anatomical studies. From the descriptions that he left it can be assumed that he was able to experiment on human and animal bodies.*

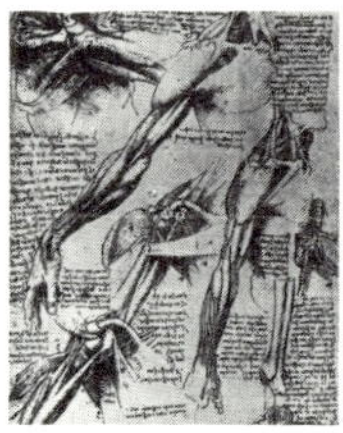

XLV - Drawing of the muscles and bones of the upper limbs - Milan, Ambrosiana - Anatomical notebooks, fol. A, fol. 14 verso - *The direct observation of cadavers was a fundamental aspect of Leonardo's scientific research. He was authorized to perform dissections after the papal bull of Pope Sixtus IV, that permitted dissection in the universities for the purpose of study.*

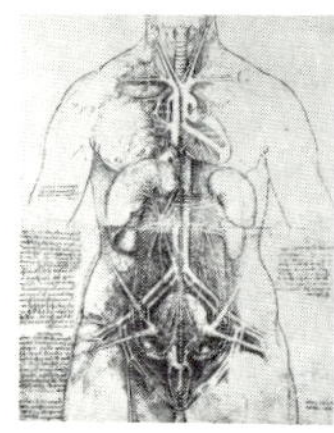

XLVI - Drawing of a woman's torso - Milan, Ambrosiana - Anatomical notebooks, Vol. I, fol. 12 recto - *Note the precision with which Leonardo depicted the internal organs, as in this drawing seen in transparency. An important characteristic of the artist's study of the various organs is the close relationship that he emphasized in the notes on the margin of the drawings between anatomy and physiology, between the structure and its function.*

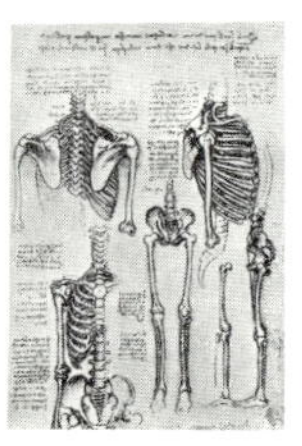

XLVII - Drawing of the skeleton of the torso and the arms - Milan, Ambrosiana - Anatomical notebooks, Sheet A, fol. 13, recto - *In the depiction of the skeleton Leonardo achieved an almost perfect representation of the various parts. He had been able to distinguish and accurately reproduce the spinal column, its curvatures, and the number of vertebrae as well as other parts of the skeleton.*

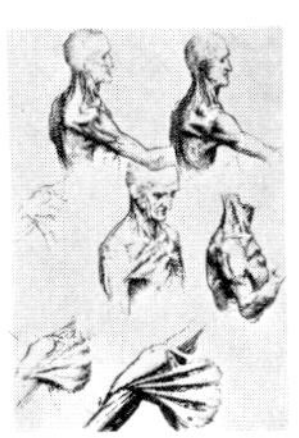

XLVIII - Drawing of the pectoral muscles - Milan, Ambrosiana - Anatomical notebooks, Sheet A, fol. 2, verso - *The hypothesis that some of Leonardo's anatomical drawings were to serve for didactic purposes seems to be confirmed. In many of the drawings, he represents the subject as seen in the various positions they assume according to the movements and their function.*

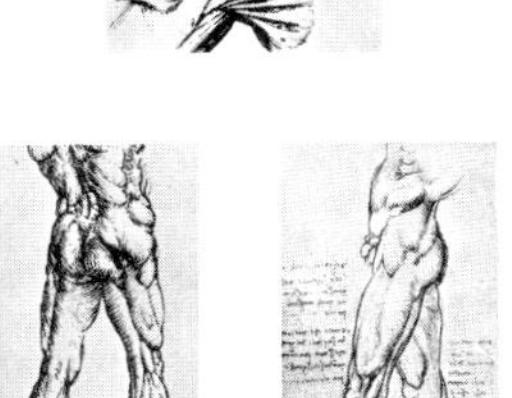

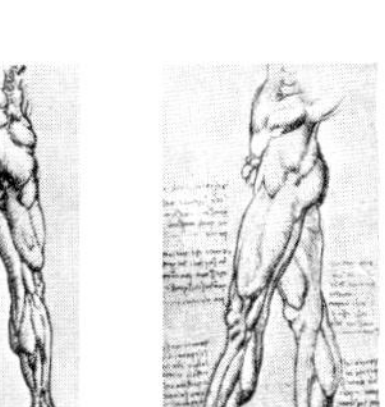

XLIX - Drawings of the back muscles and of the lower limbs - Milan, Ambrosiana - Anatomical notebooks, Vol. V, fol. 22, recto - *Leonardo did not at first intend a scientific study of anatomy, but he began his studies in order to acquire a more solid and realistic base for his art. This can be seen in the precision of some of his anatomical drawings where it is difficult to distinguish the work of the artist from that of the scientist.*

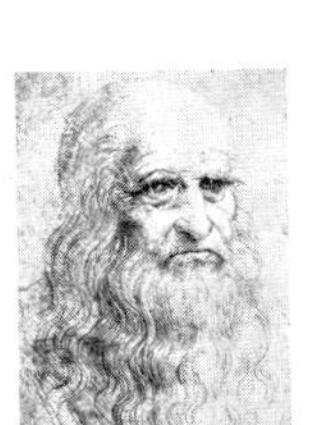

L - Self-portrait - Turin, Biblioteca Reale - *This self-portrait, the best known of the artist, is without a doubt the one which most faithfully reflects the descriptions of Leonardo that were made by his contemporaries. They all spoke of his expressive face, his limpid eyes, his intense and profound look, his refined and at the same time sweet and majestic features.*

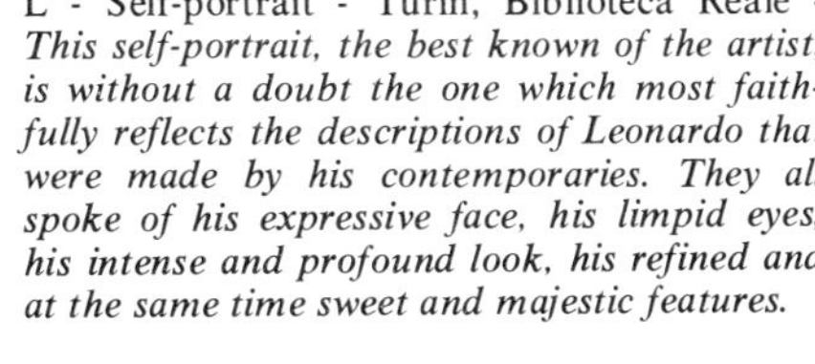

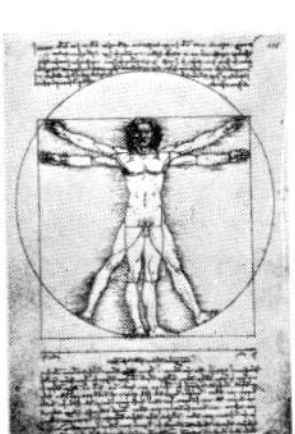

LI - The rule of proportions - Venice, Academy - *From Leonardo's important anatomical researches there emerged an ultimate important teaching: the principle of relationships and proportions. After having demonstrated that the lip is a 12th part of the face and a 112th part of the entire body, he warned that one should use science only as a base for constructing the work of art, and not as an end in itself.*

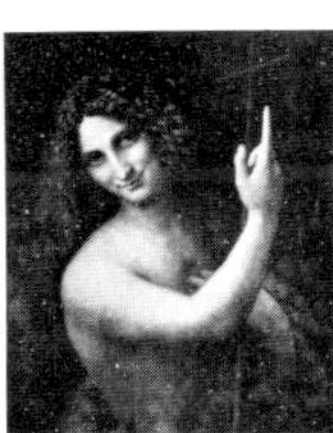

LII - St. John the Baptist - Paris, Musée du Louvre - *It is difficult to date this painting, though it is probable that it was made during Leonardo's stay in Rome. We know for certain that the artist brought the painting with him to France and, as written in a document of the period, he delighted in showing it to Cardinal Luigi d'Aragón, who had visited Leonardo at Cloux, with a few other works that were particularly dear to him.*

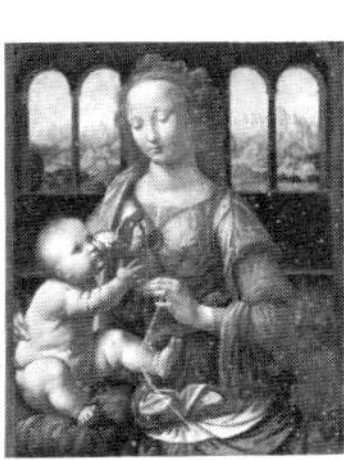

LIII - Virgin and Child - Munich, Alte Pinakothek - *This work is often identified with one of the two "Vergini Marie" that Leonardo annotated in a margin of a drawing in 1478. The painting is still influenced by Verrocchio's style in the solid structure of the figures, but one can already observe new subtleties in the light on the clothes, on the flesh, and on the flowers.*

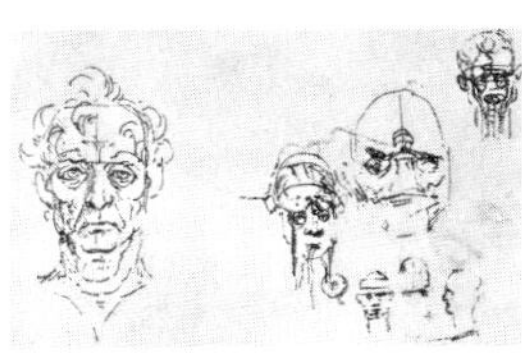

LIV - Drawings of faces with eyeglasses - Anatomical notebooks, V, fol. 6, recto - *Leonardo was very interested in the study of the eye, and he was able to describe its structure in terms that are valid today. He described the structure of the retina, the optic nerve, and other specific parts. He was able to indicate almost exactly the nature of presbyopia, demonstrating the correct function of eyeglasses.*

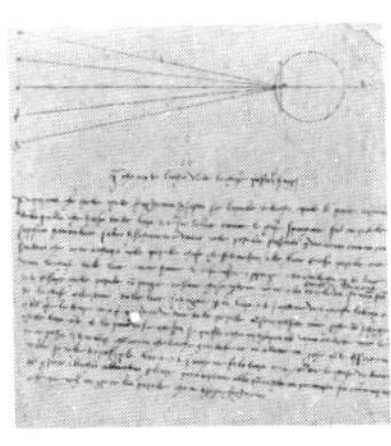

LV - Drawing and description of the functioning of the eye - Milan, Ambrosiana - Atlantic Codex, fol. 85, verso - *Leonardo studied the eye not only for the interest that this organ could stimulate due to its complexity, but also, as described on this page, for its symbolic value as the transmitter of images to the mind, being, therefore, man's guide to knowledge.*

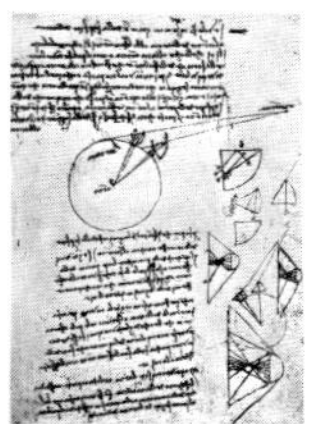

LVI - Study for the measurement of the earth from the surface to the center - London, Royal Coll. of Windsor, no. 19148 - *Astronomy attracted Leonardo's attention, partly due to certain celestial phenomena that occurred during his life. Though he never pursued a systematic study in this field, he was able to arrive at certain surprising conclusions for his time, such as the concept of the sun's being larger than the earth.*

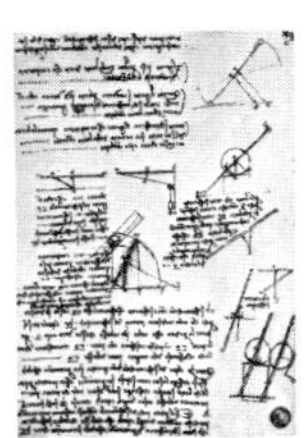

LVII - Study of mechanics - Venice, Academy - *This page is of primary importance in understanding the systematic treatment of Leonardo's mechanics. He divided the entire range of the material into various books: the first was to treat the problems of weights; the others, the study of statics, gravity, motion, and finally percussion or the theory of impact.*

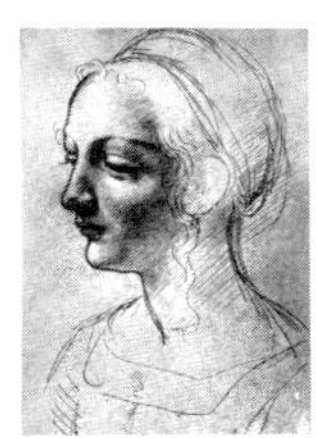

LVIII - Drawing of the head of a young woman - London, Royal Coll. of Windsor - *It has been said that for Leonardo drawing was his ideal form of writing. It was the means by which he transcribed at every moment and in every technique (pencil, charcoal, pen and ink, silverpoint) his ideas, his deductions, his creations. When he thought of a project for a sculpture he made 19 drawings for 19 possible positions of the sculpture.*

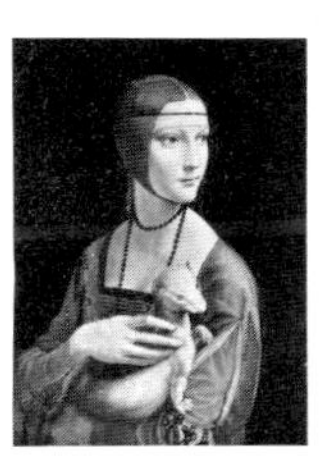

LIX - The Lady with an Ermine - Karkow, Czartorisky Museum - *The attribution of this portrait to Leonardo—so radical in the form of the body, so intense in the expression of the face—is not unanimously accepted. The work can be dated about 1490. The person has been variously identified as Cecilia Gallerani or Beatrice d'Este, the wife of Ludovico il Moro.*

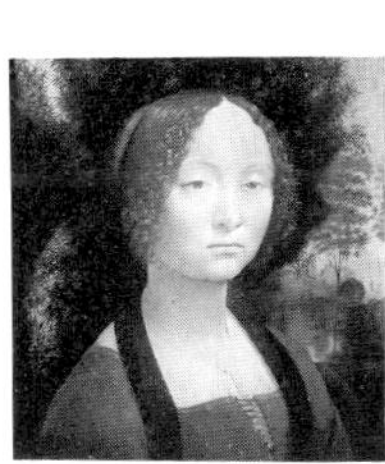

LX - Portrait of Ginevra Benci - Washington, National Gallery - *It is commonly identified as the portrait of Ginevra Benci, mentioned by Vasari as a "beautiful thing." The attribution of the work to Leonardo, previously often debated, is now generally accepted. The work has been cut on the lowes part where the hands were painted, perhaps crossed one over the other as in the* Mona Lisa.

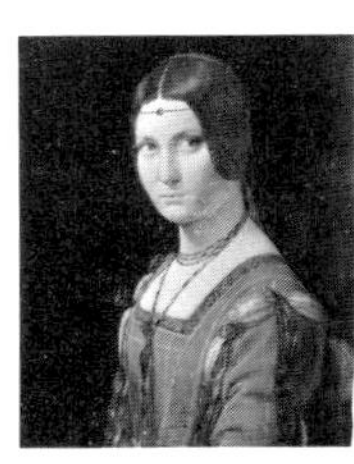

LXI - La Belle Ferronière - Paris, Musée du Louvre - *A very particular characteristic of Leonardo's painting is his handling of the* sfumato *with which he softened the faces, veiled the surfaces, modulated the shadows so as to bestow to his paintings that languor and that evanescence of light and forms that have always fascinated the viewers of his paintings, especially in his portraits of women.*

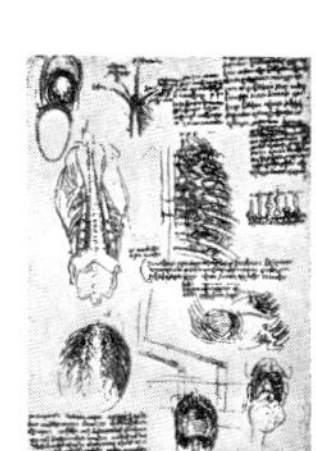

LXII - Anatomical studies on the myology of an ox - Anatomical notebooks, Vol. IV, fol. 2, verso - *Leonardo had studied the anatomy of animals during the formulation of certain art works, such as in the drawings and notes on horses made during the preparation of the equestrian monument to Francesco Sforza. These studies, which resulted from his passion for research, became the precursor of comparative anatomy.*

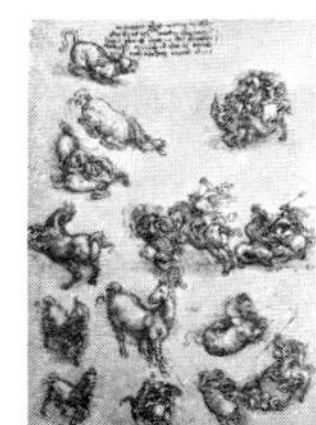

LXIII - Study of a battle between a horse and a dragon - London, Royal Coll. of Windsor, no. 12331 - *This is one of the documents that best reflect the multiple aspects of Leonardo's genius: the artist who exhibits his pictorial virtuosity, the scientist who observes and studies the animal's movements, the poet's fantasy that dictated the theme.*

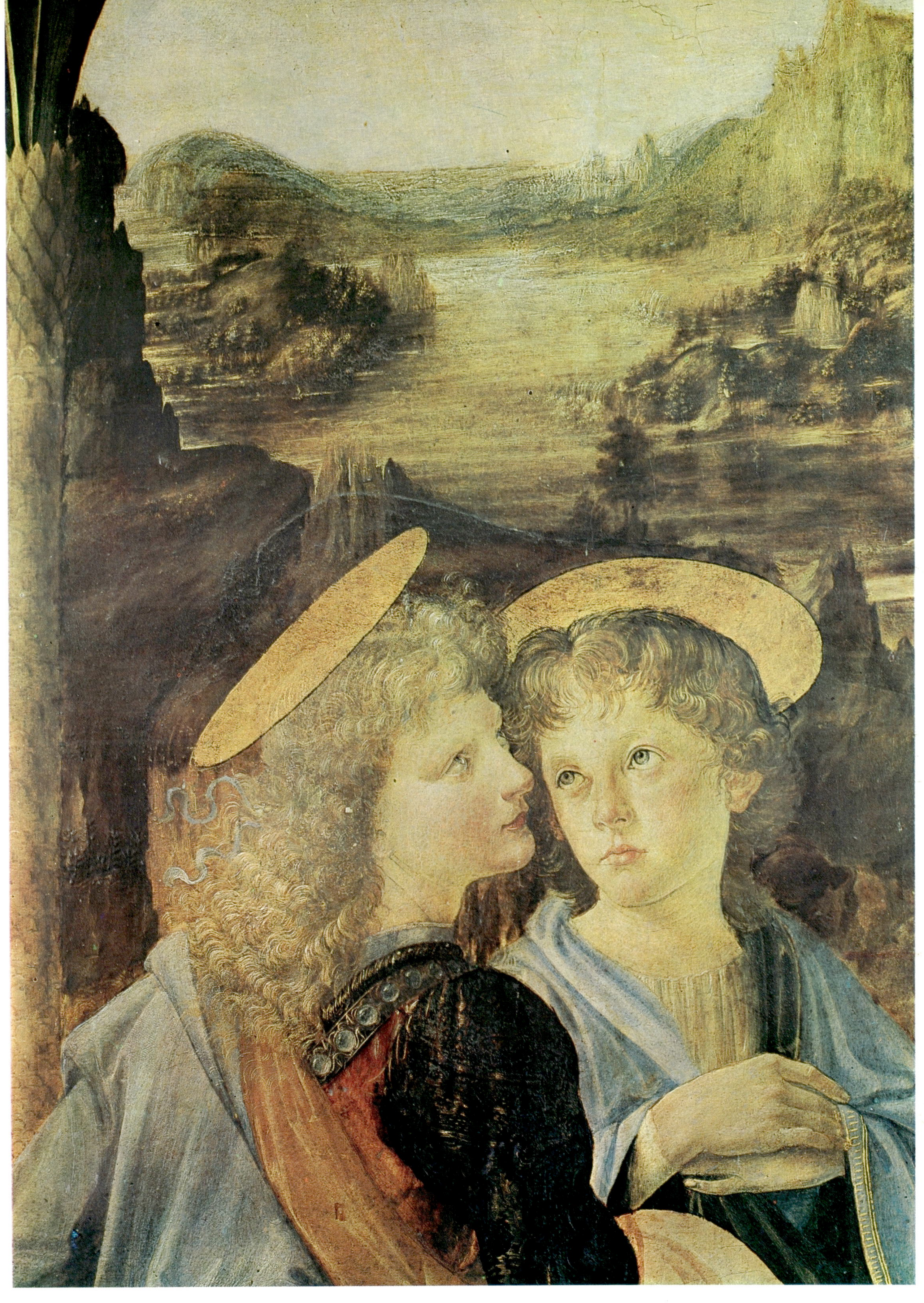

I

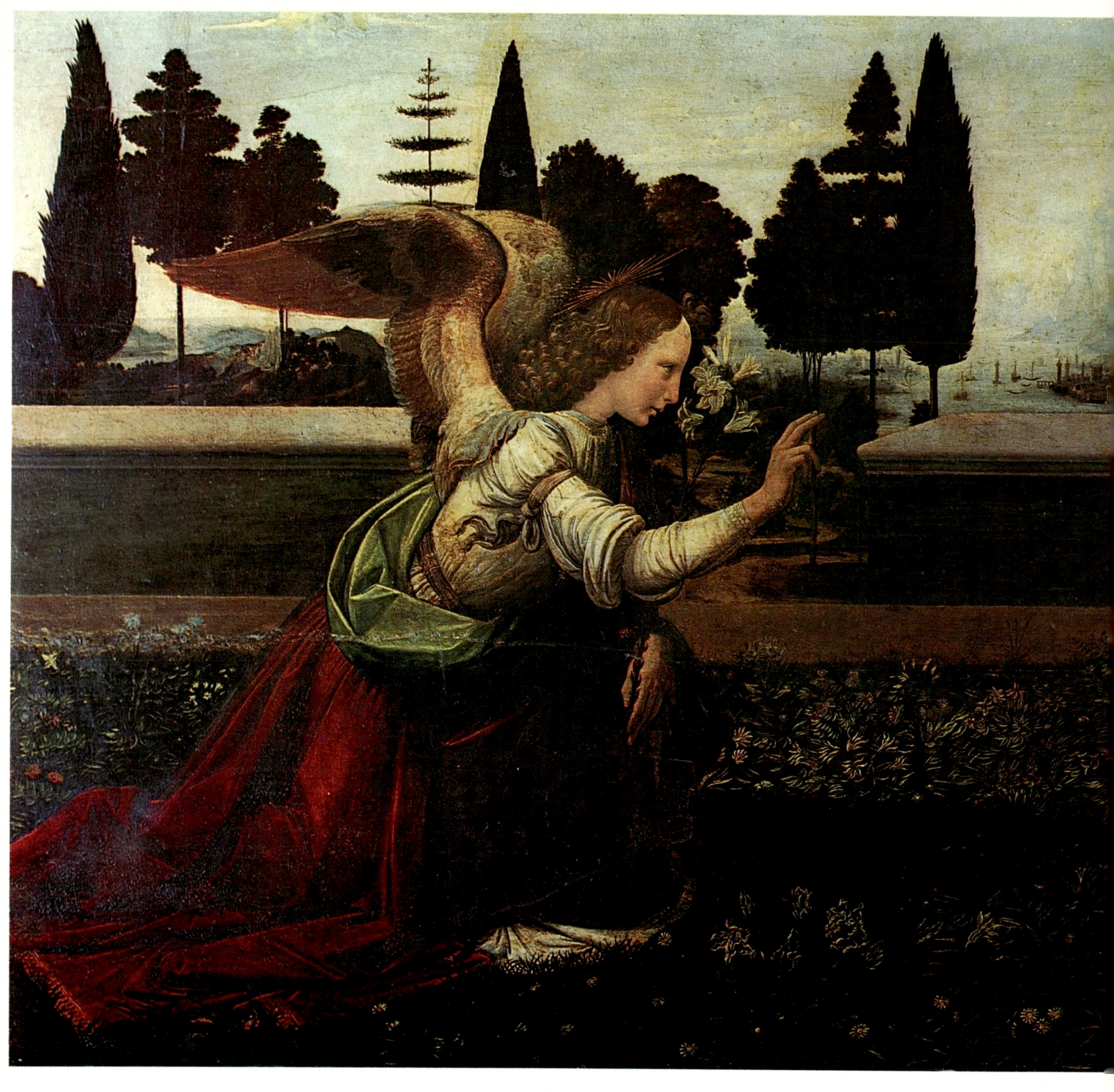

II

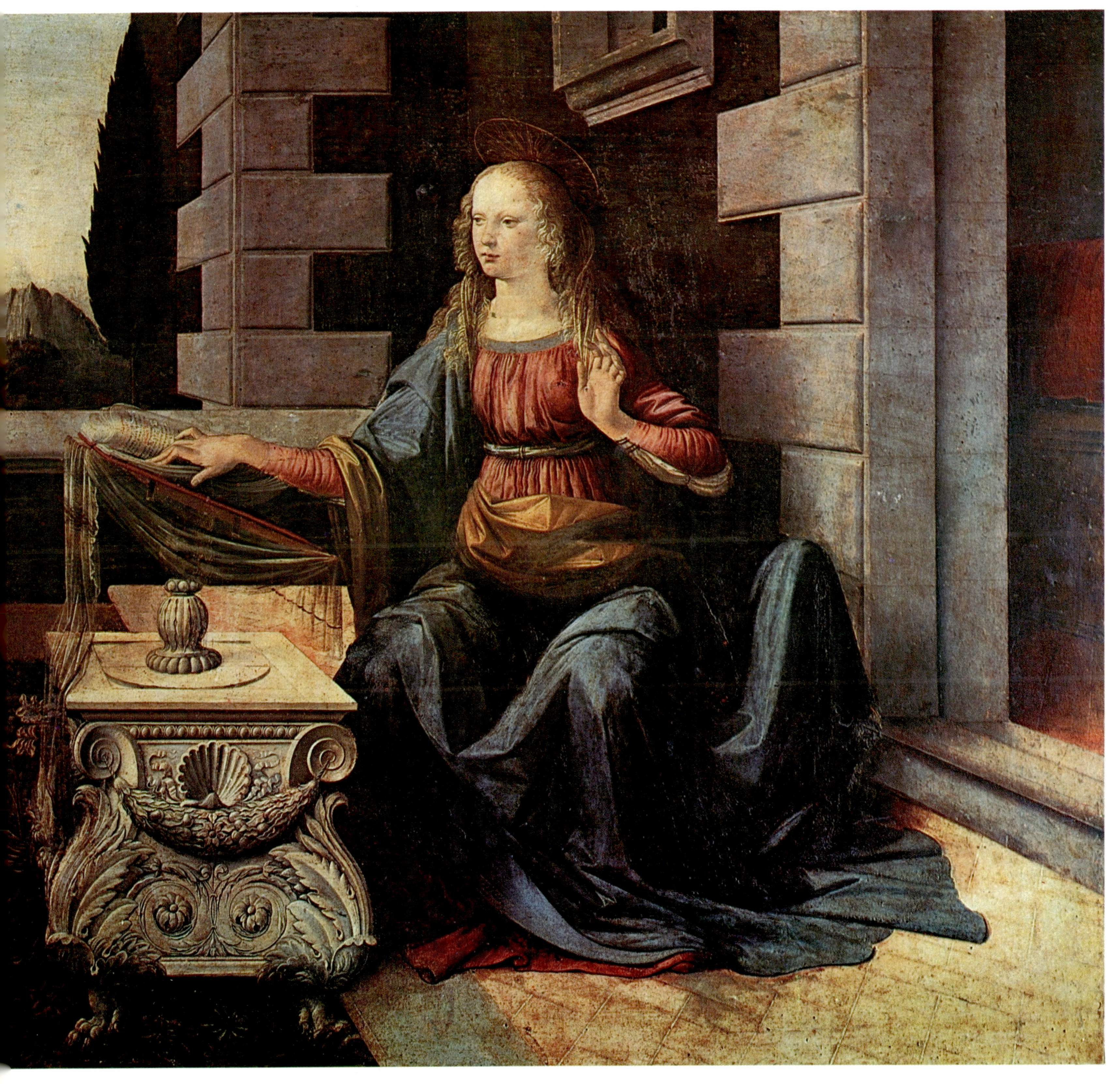

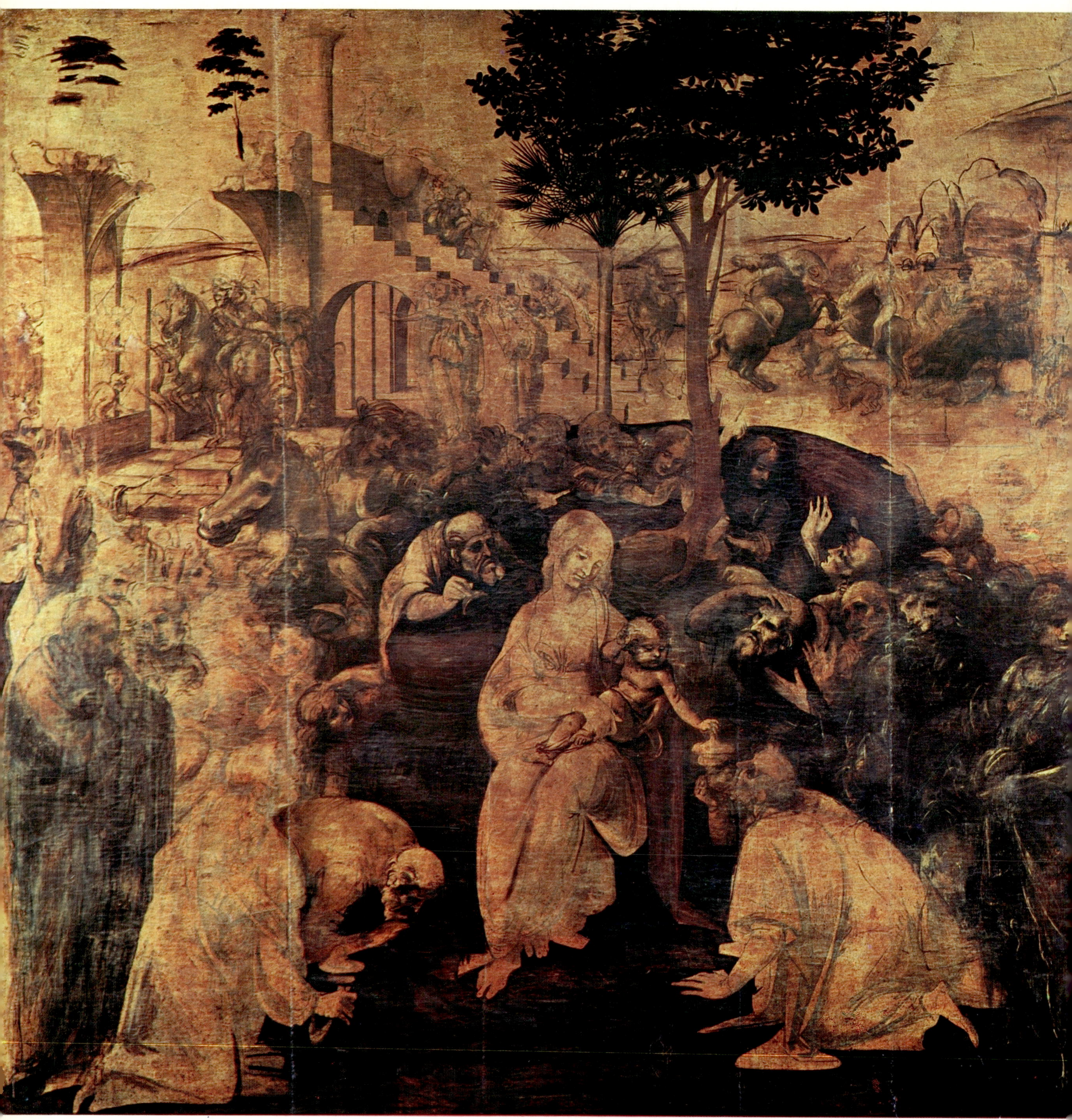

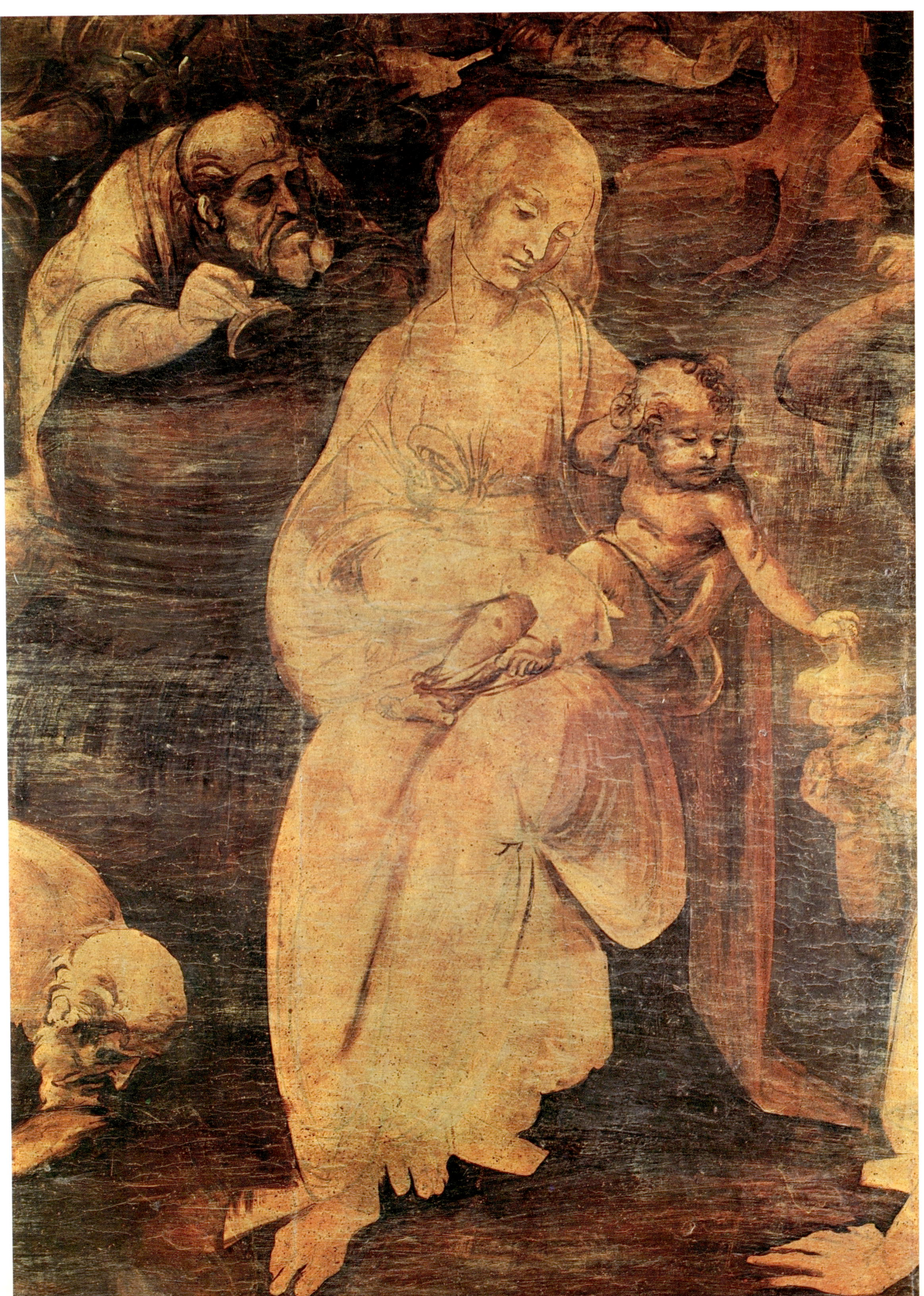

V

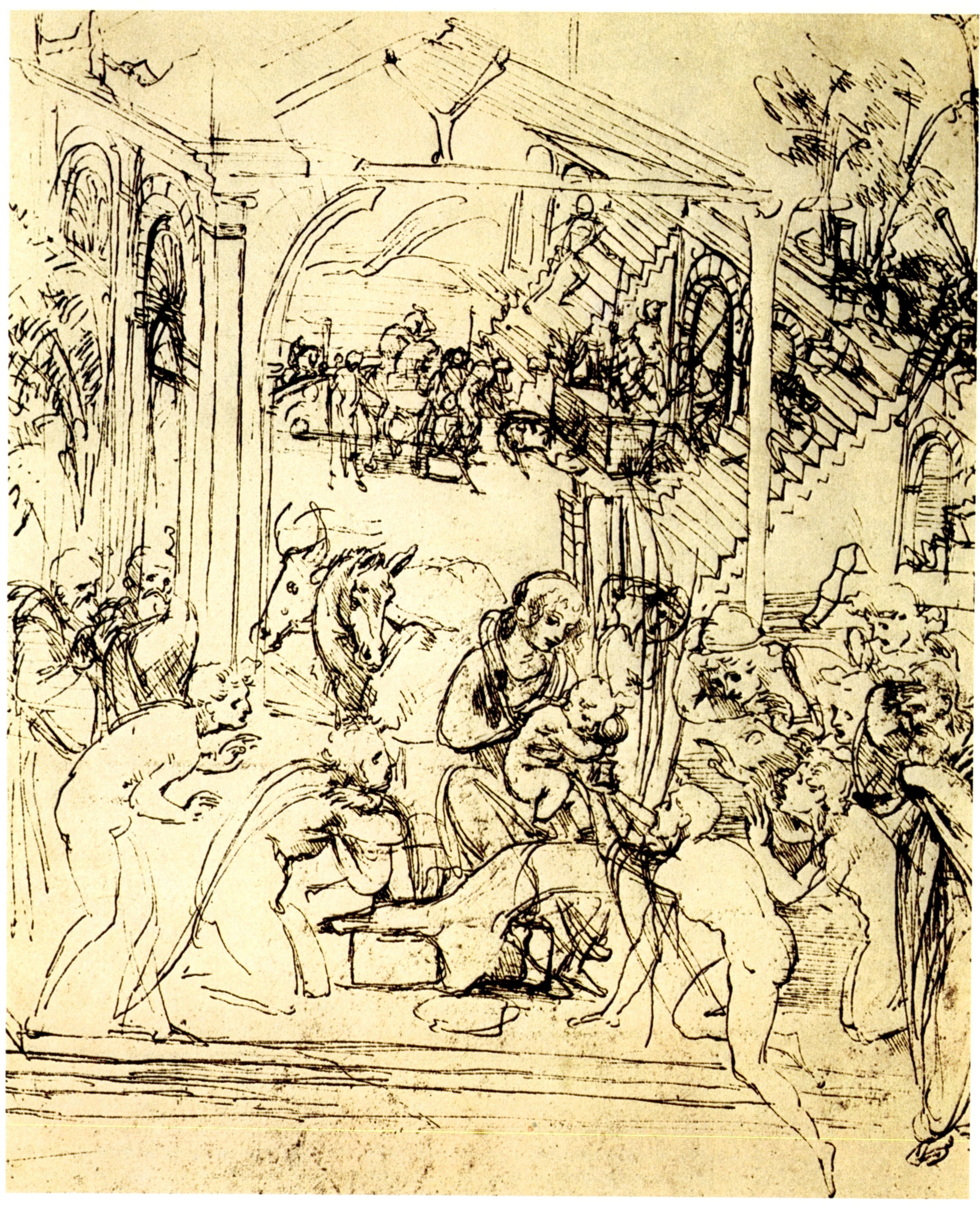

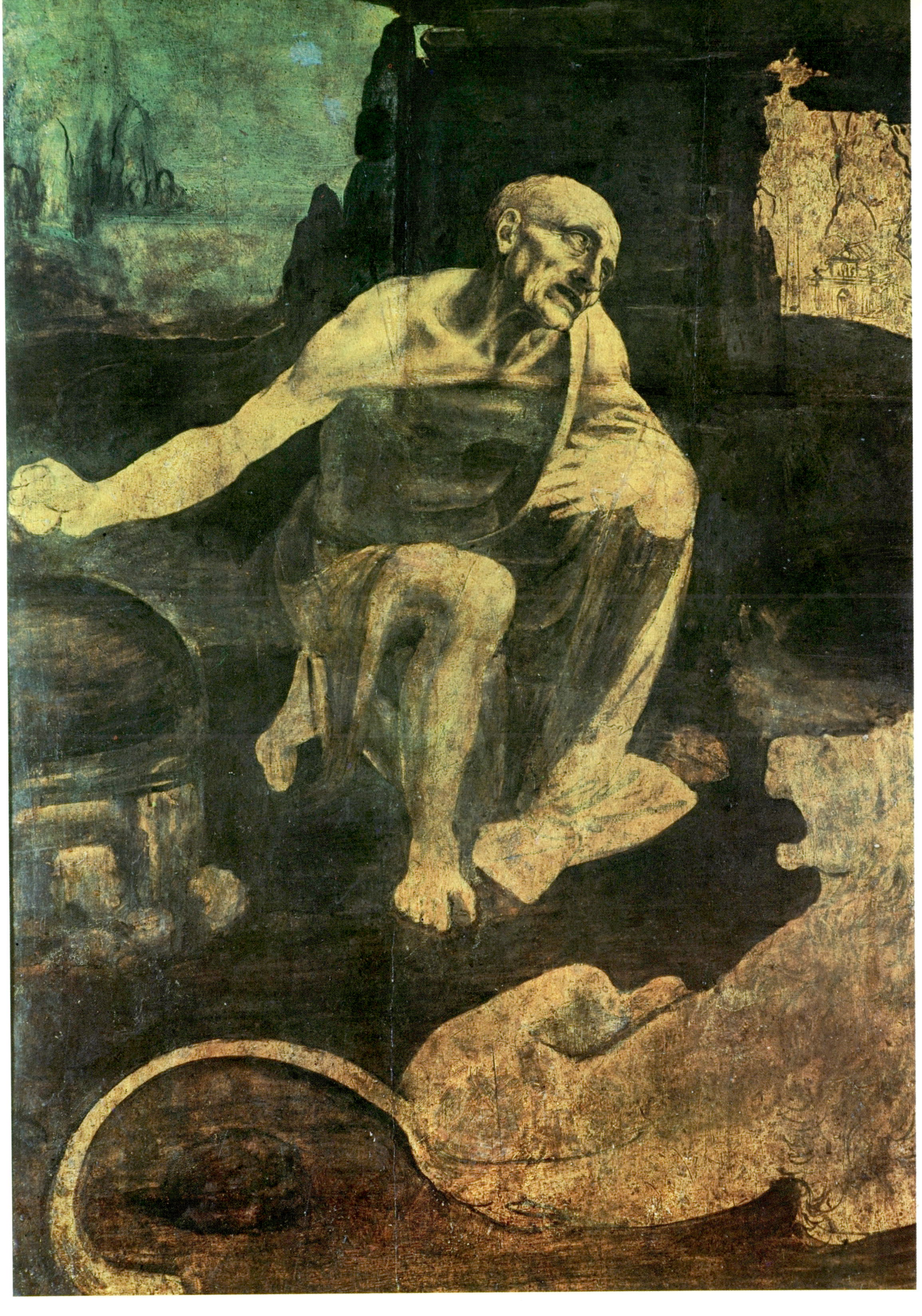

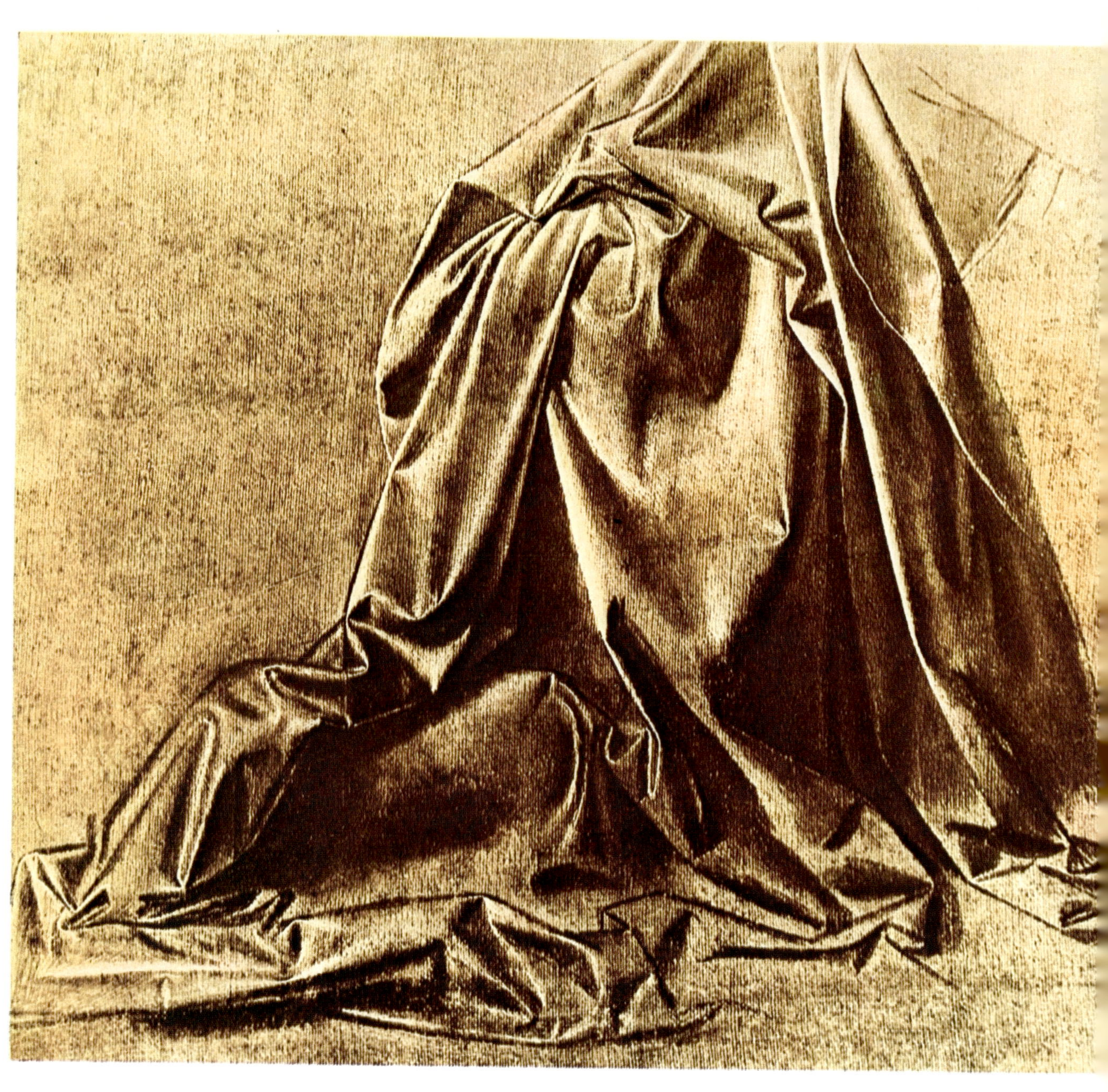

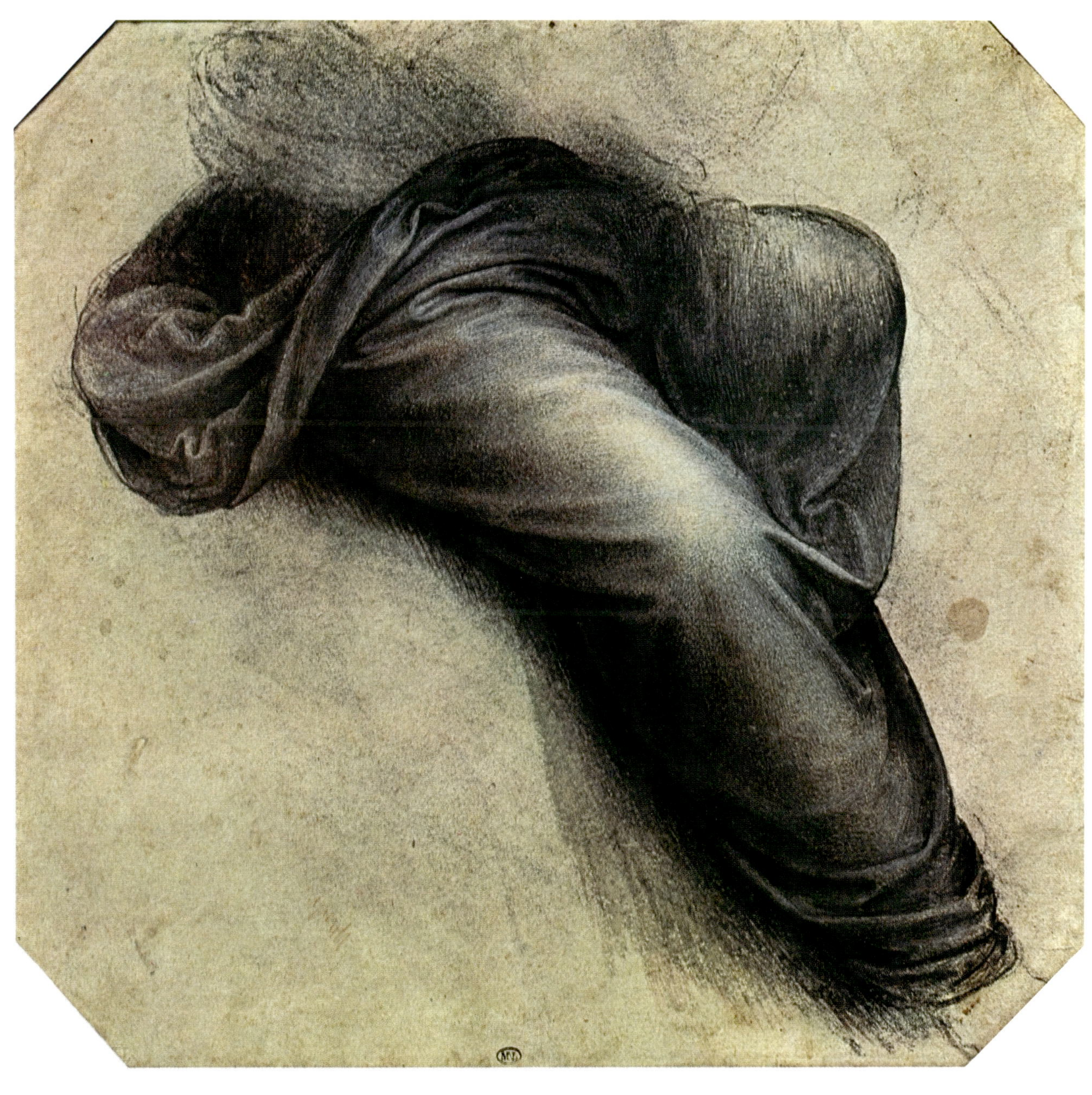

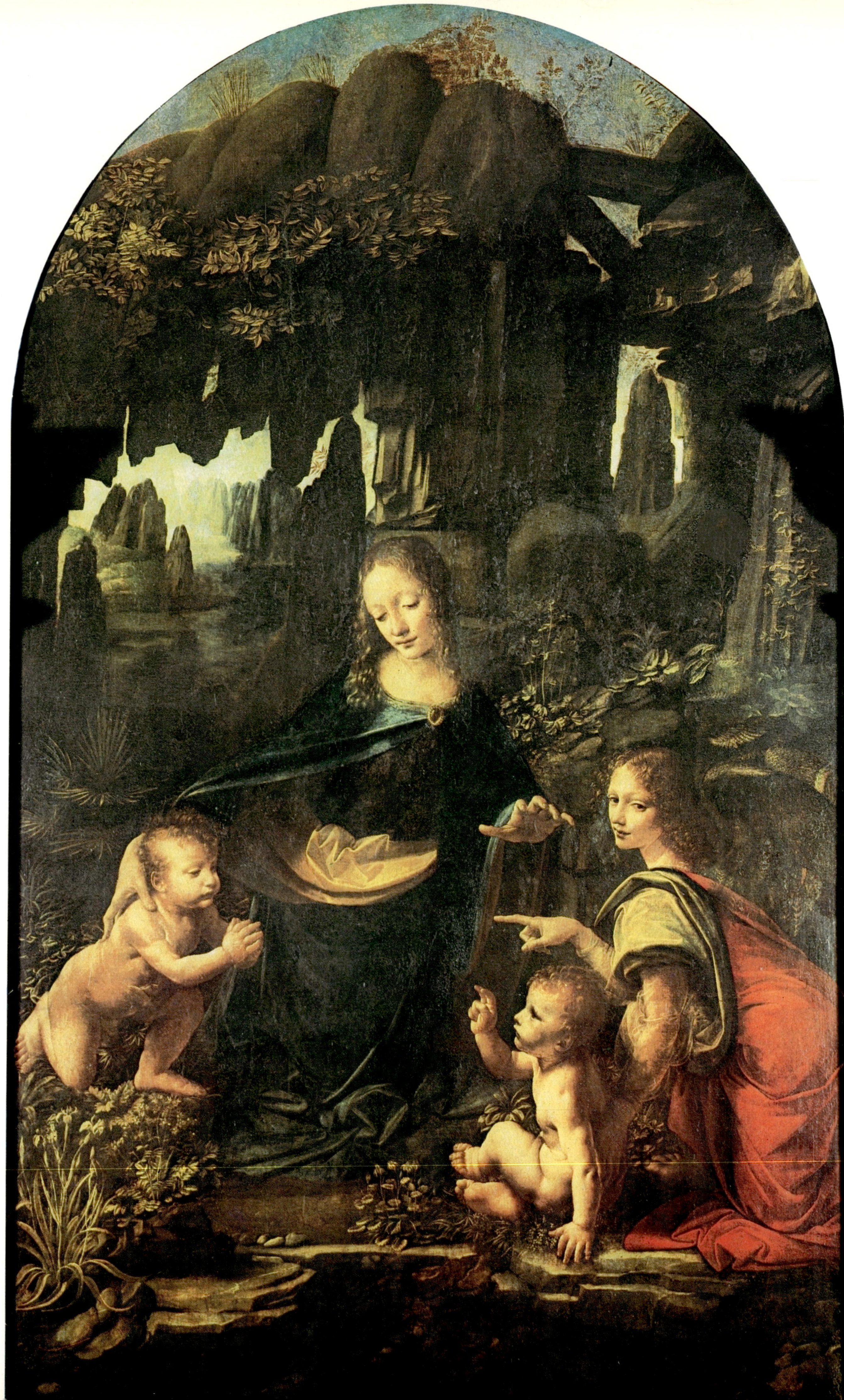

X

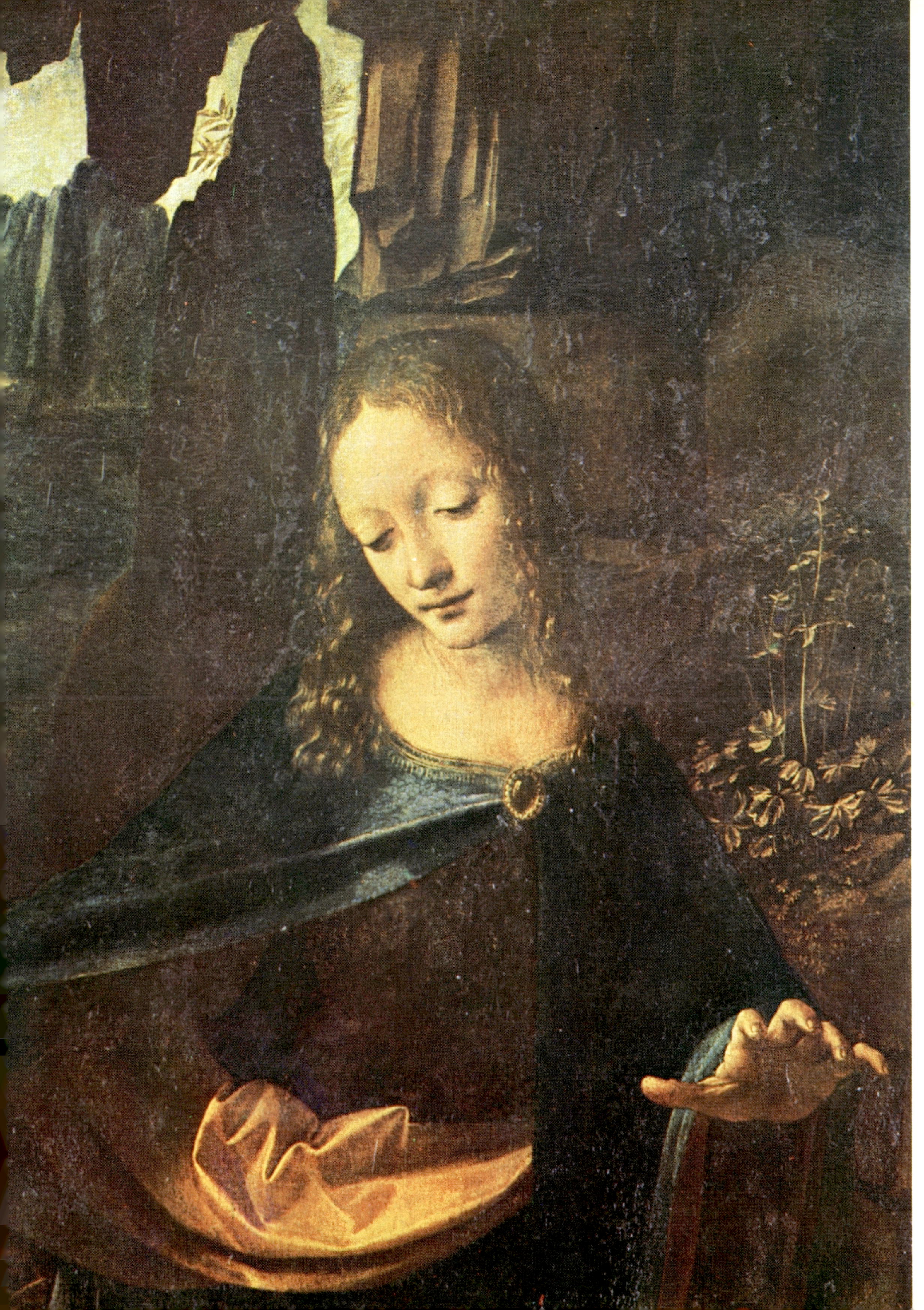

XI

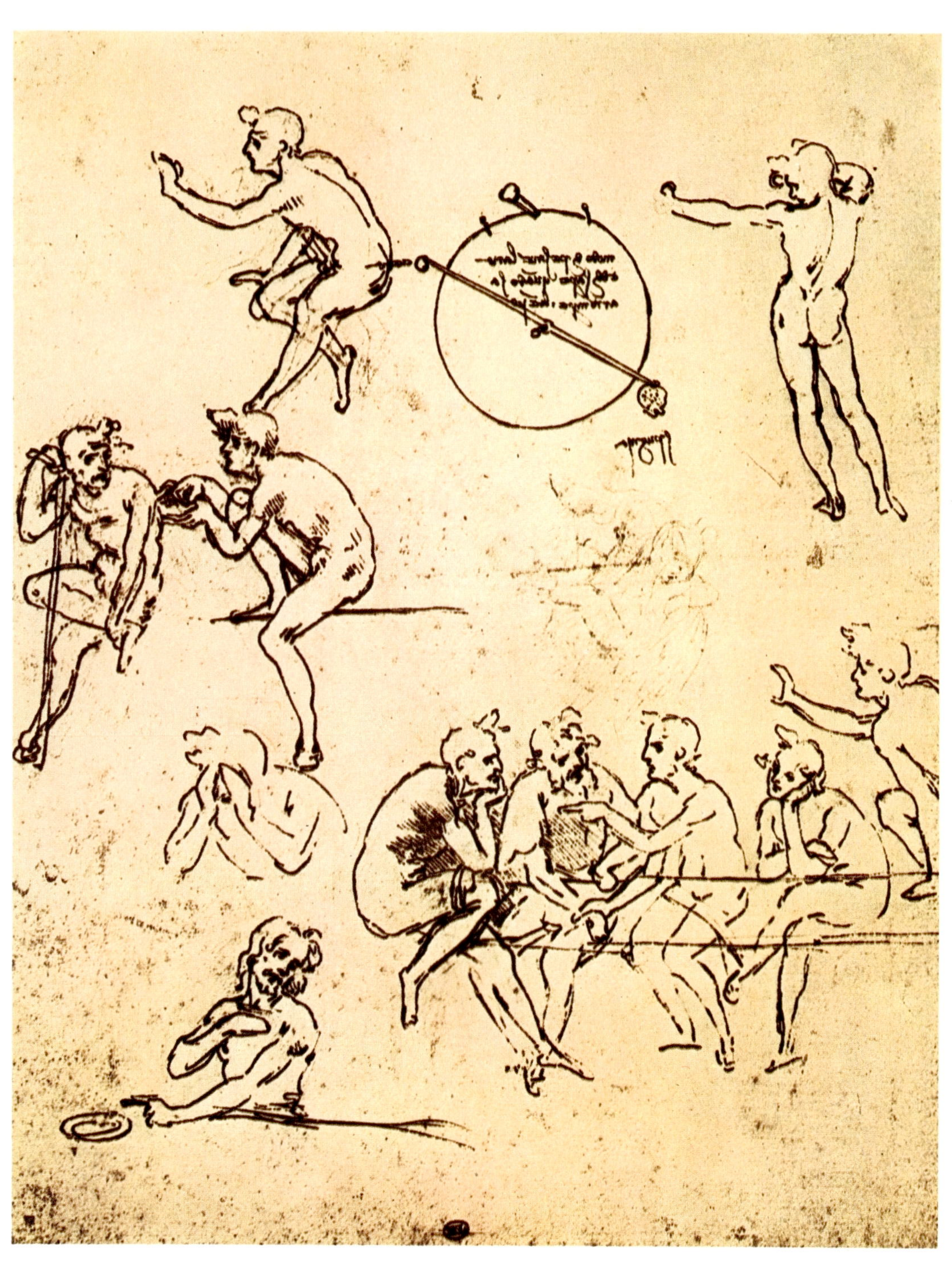

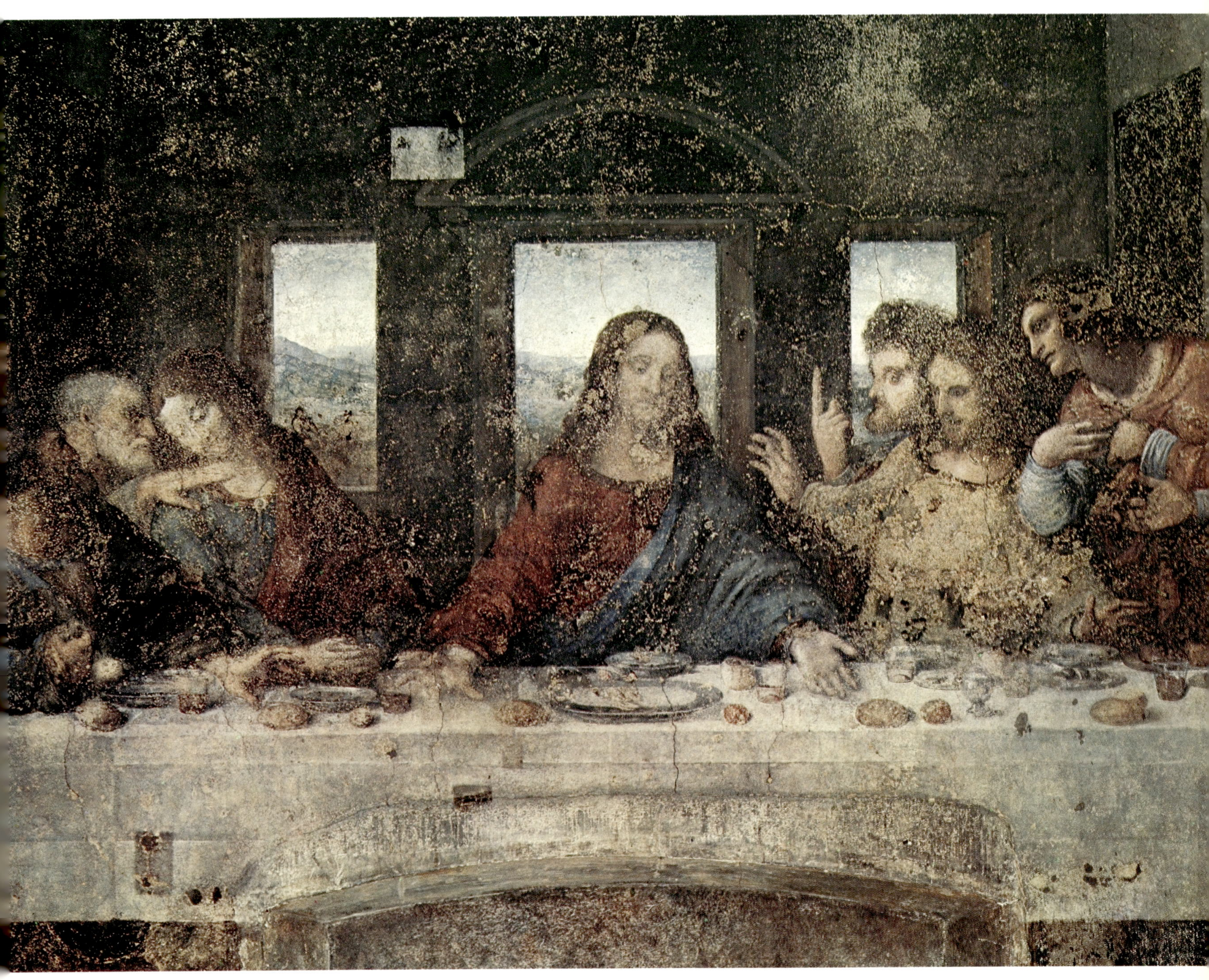

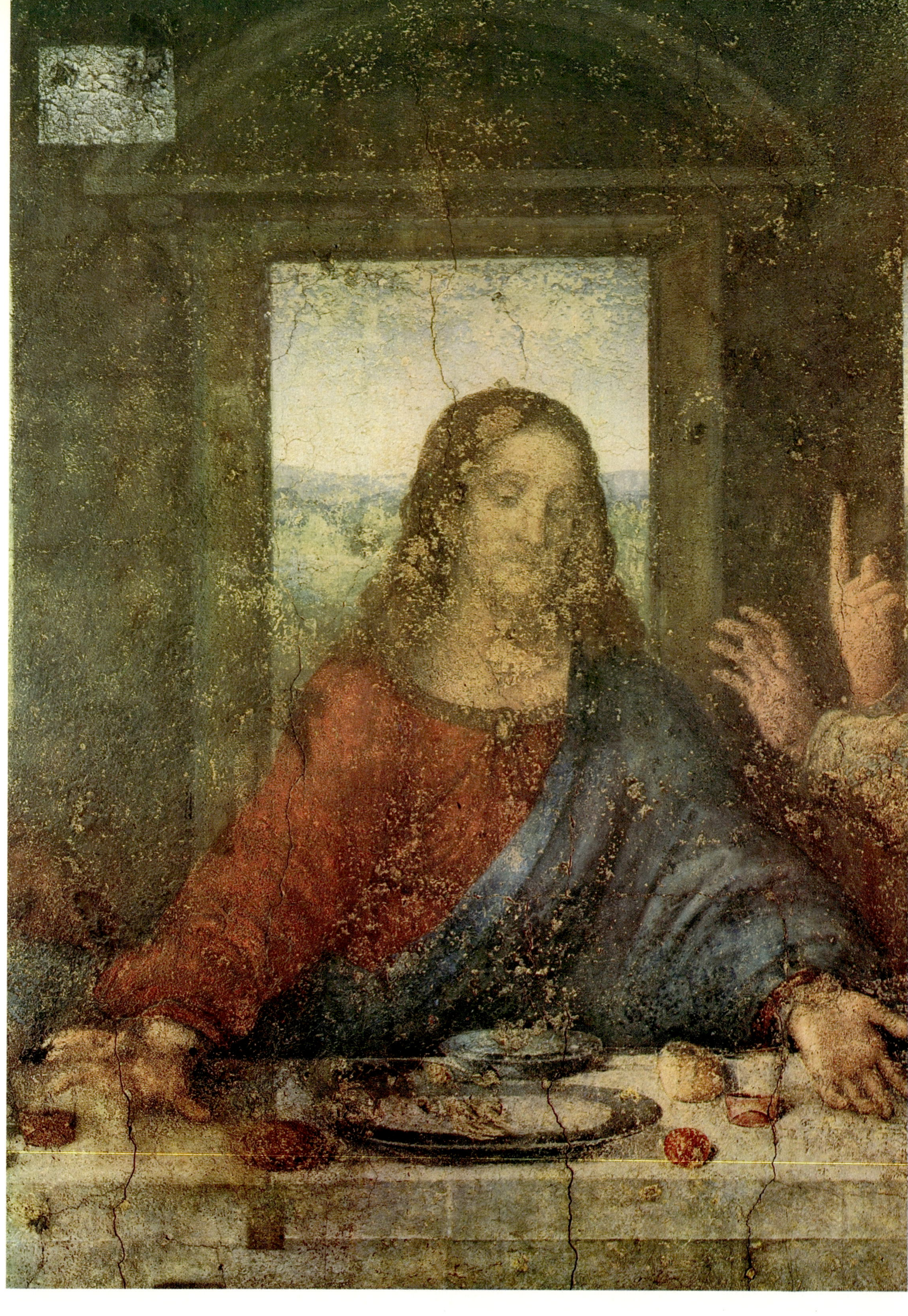

XIV

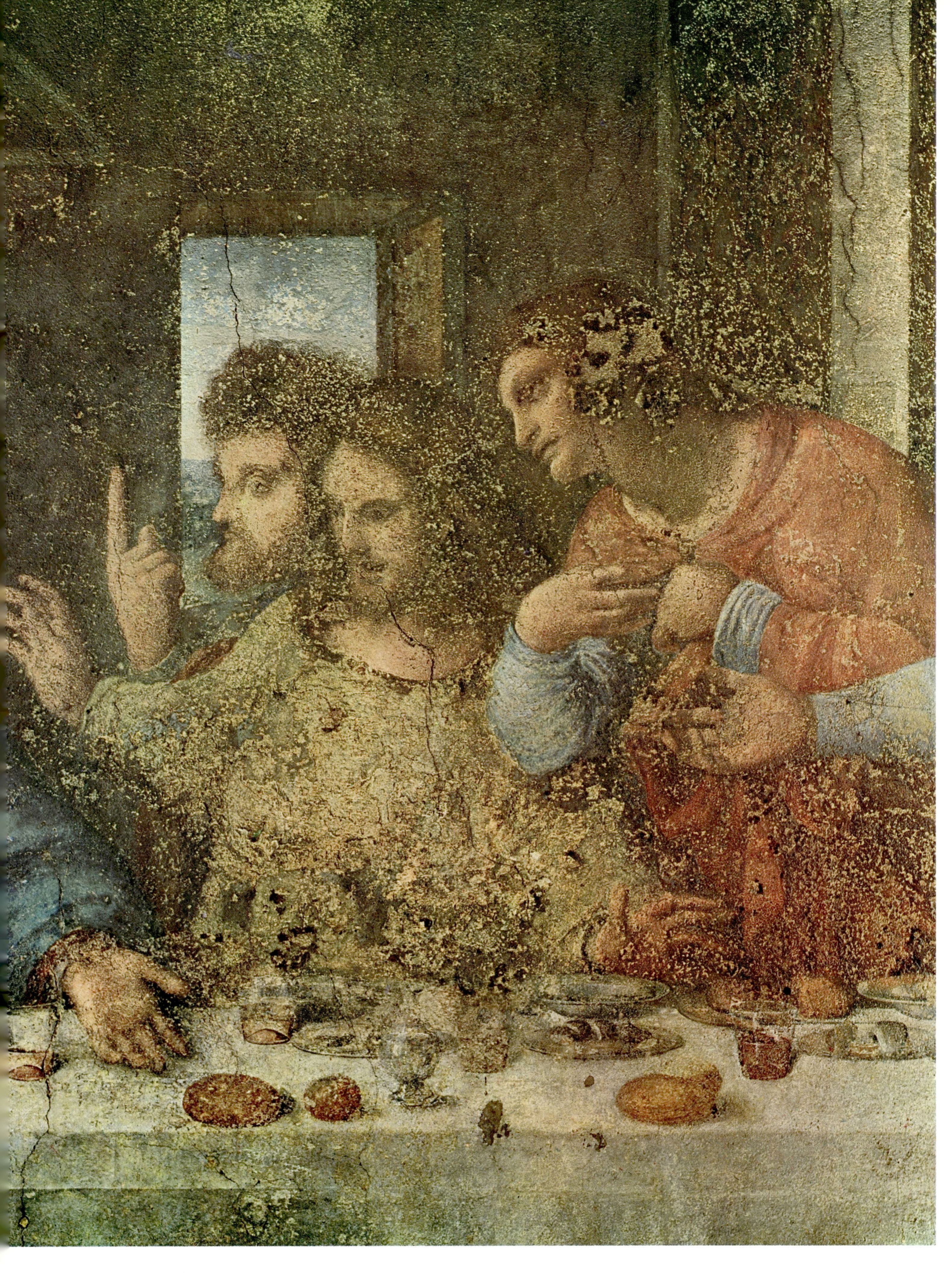

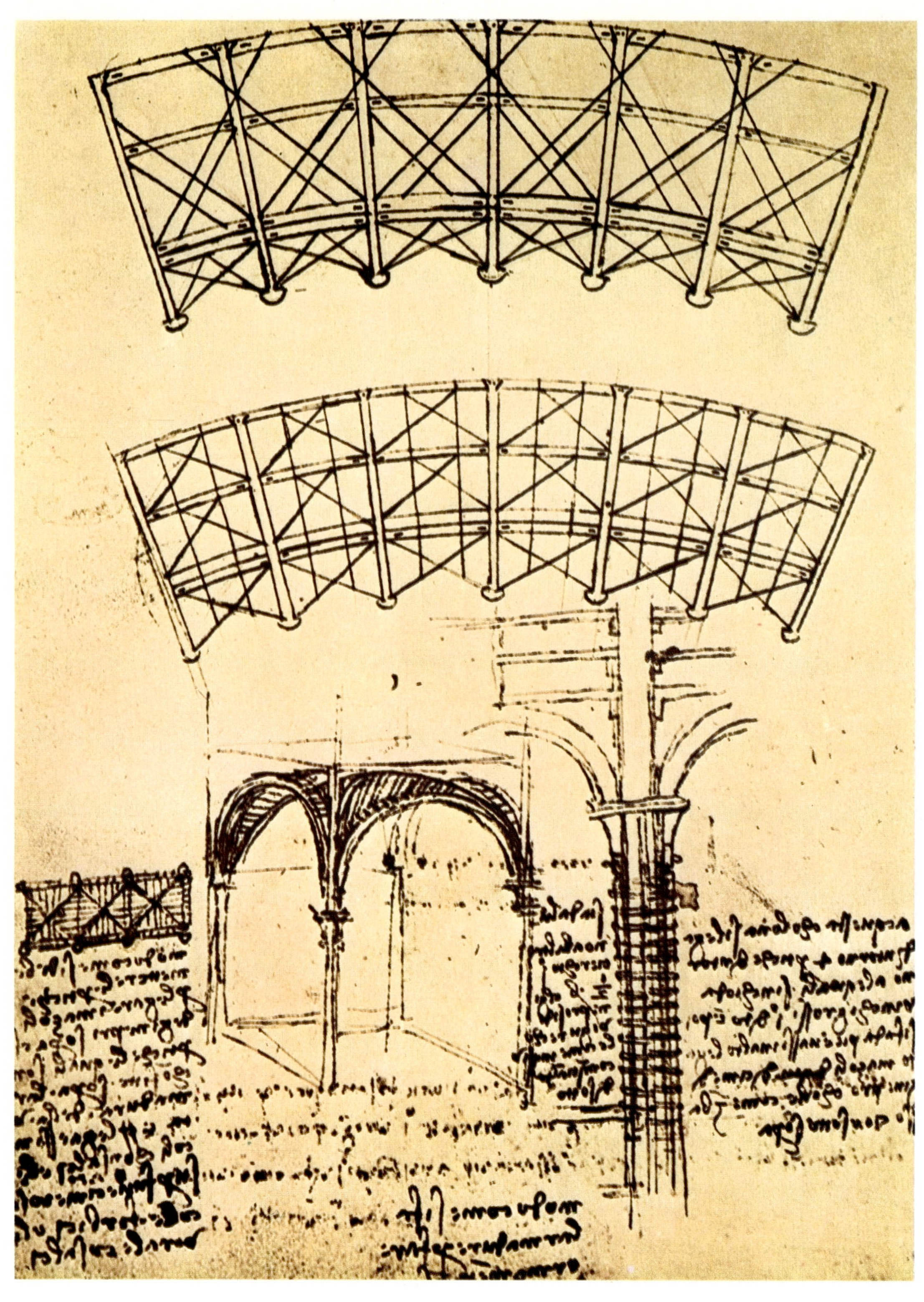

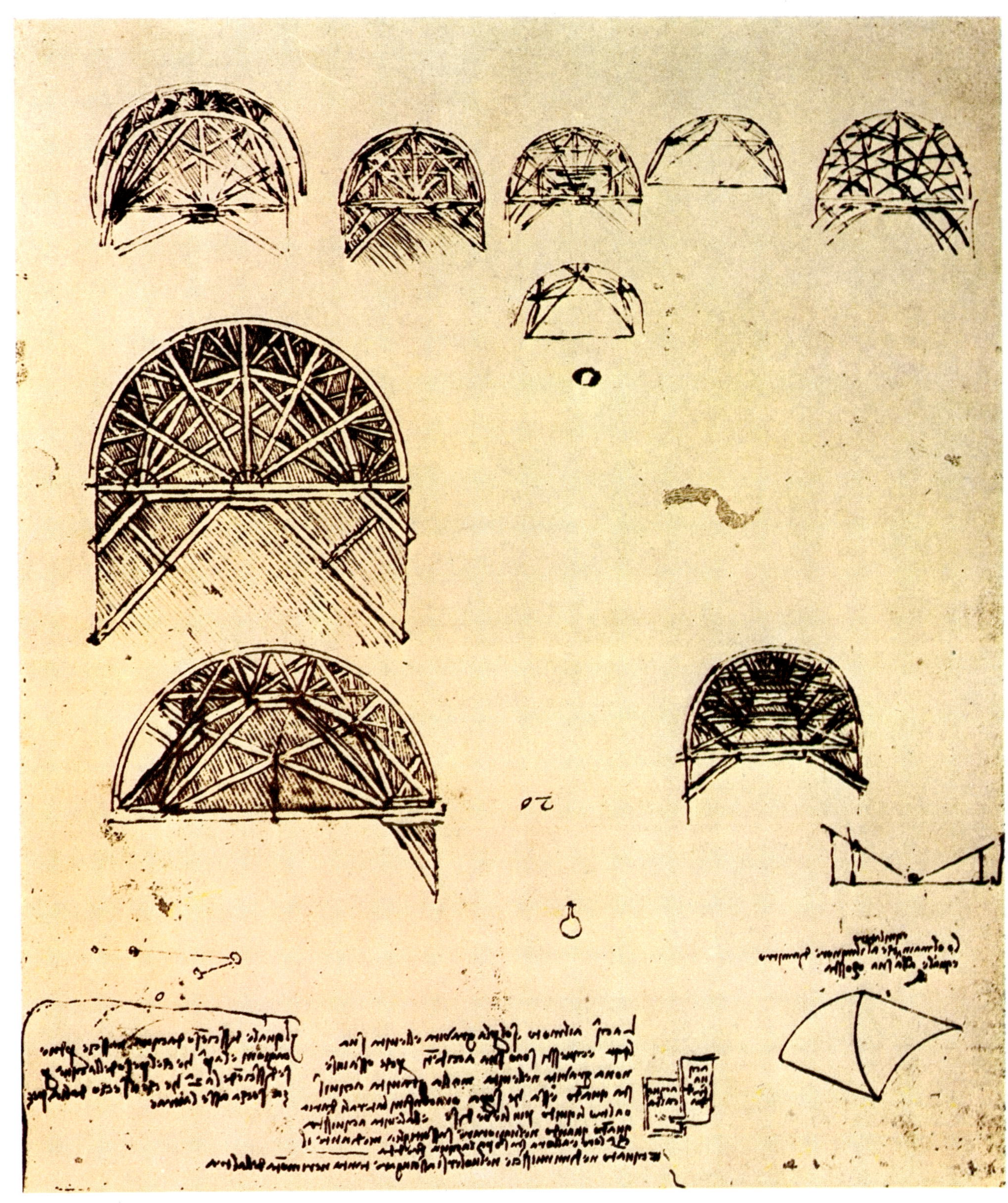

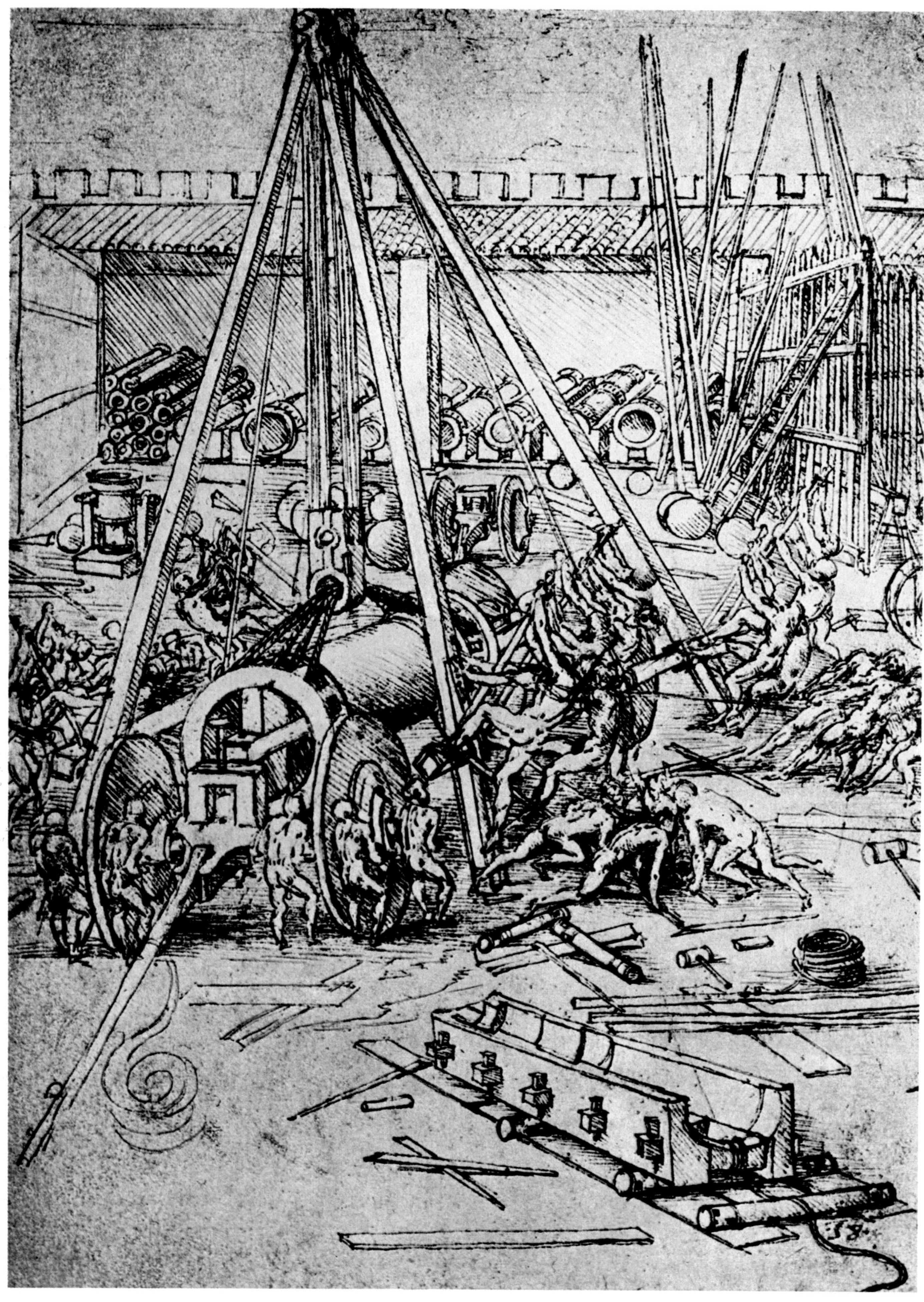

XVIII

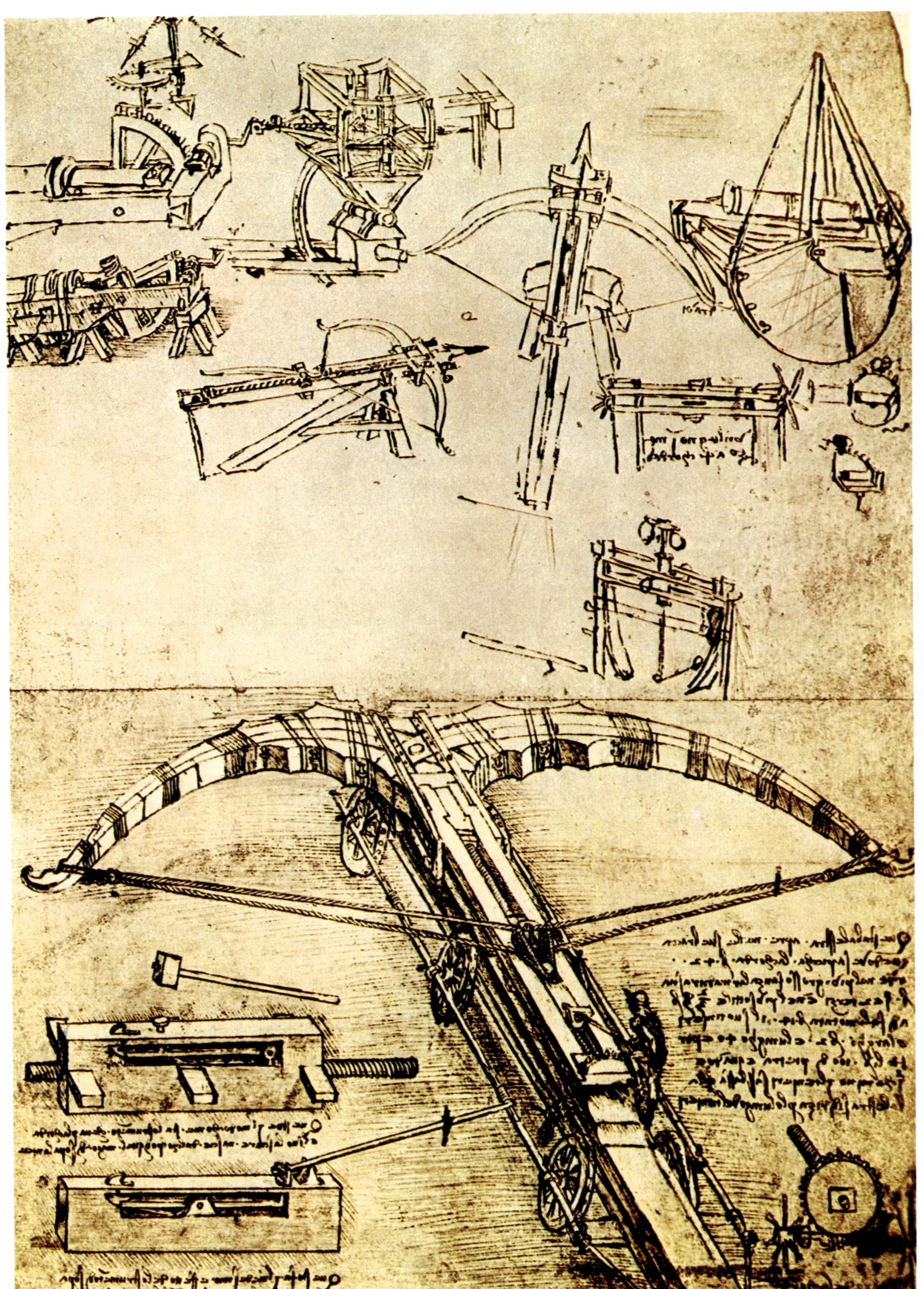

XX

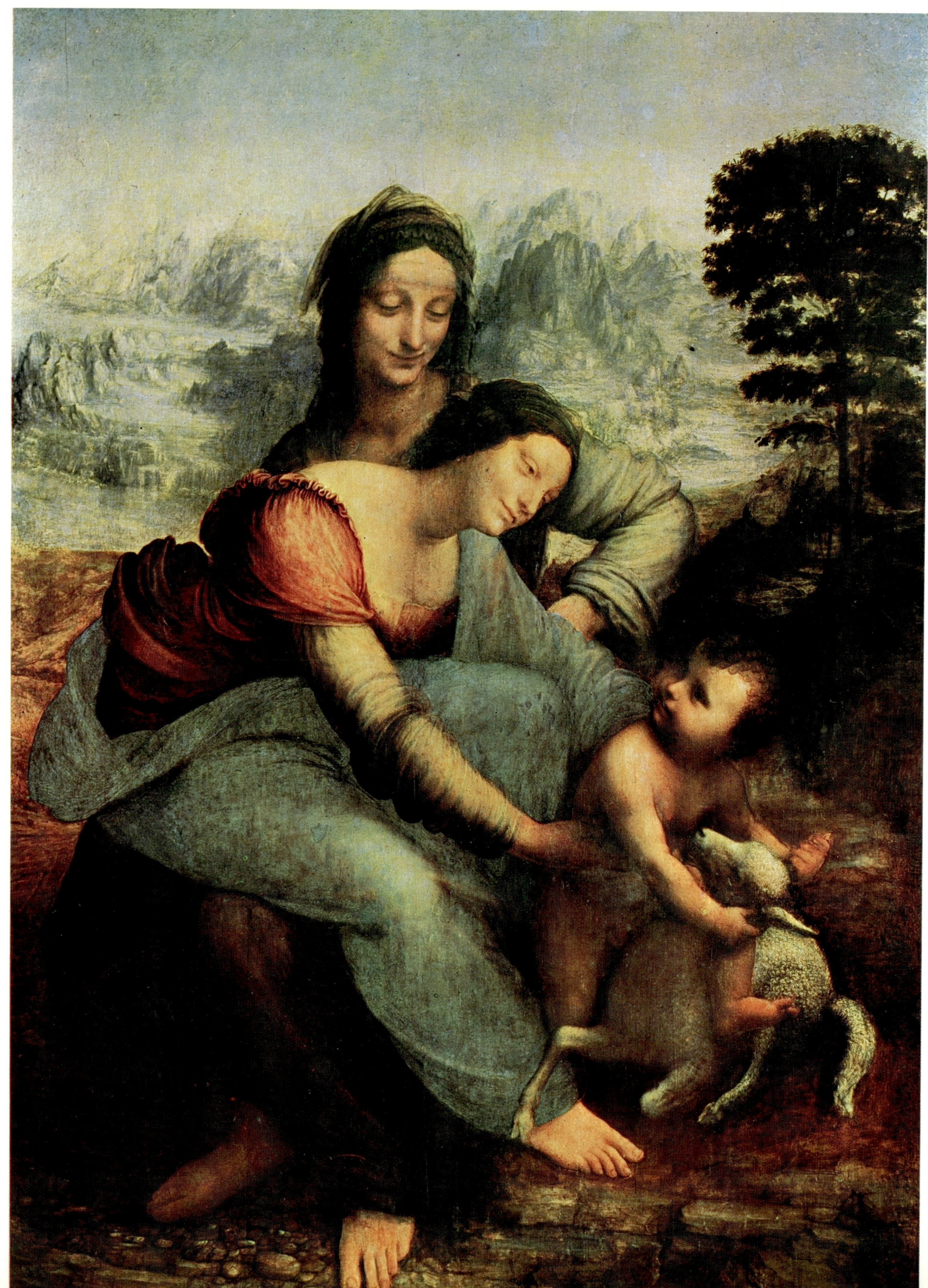

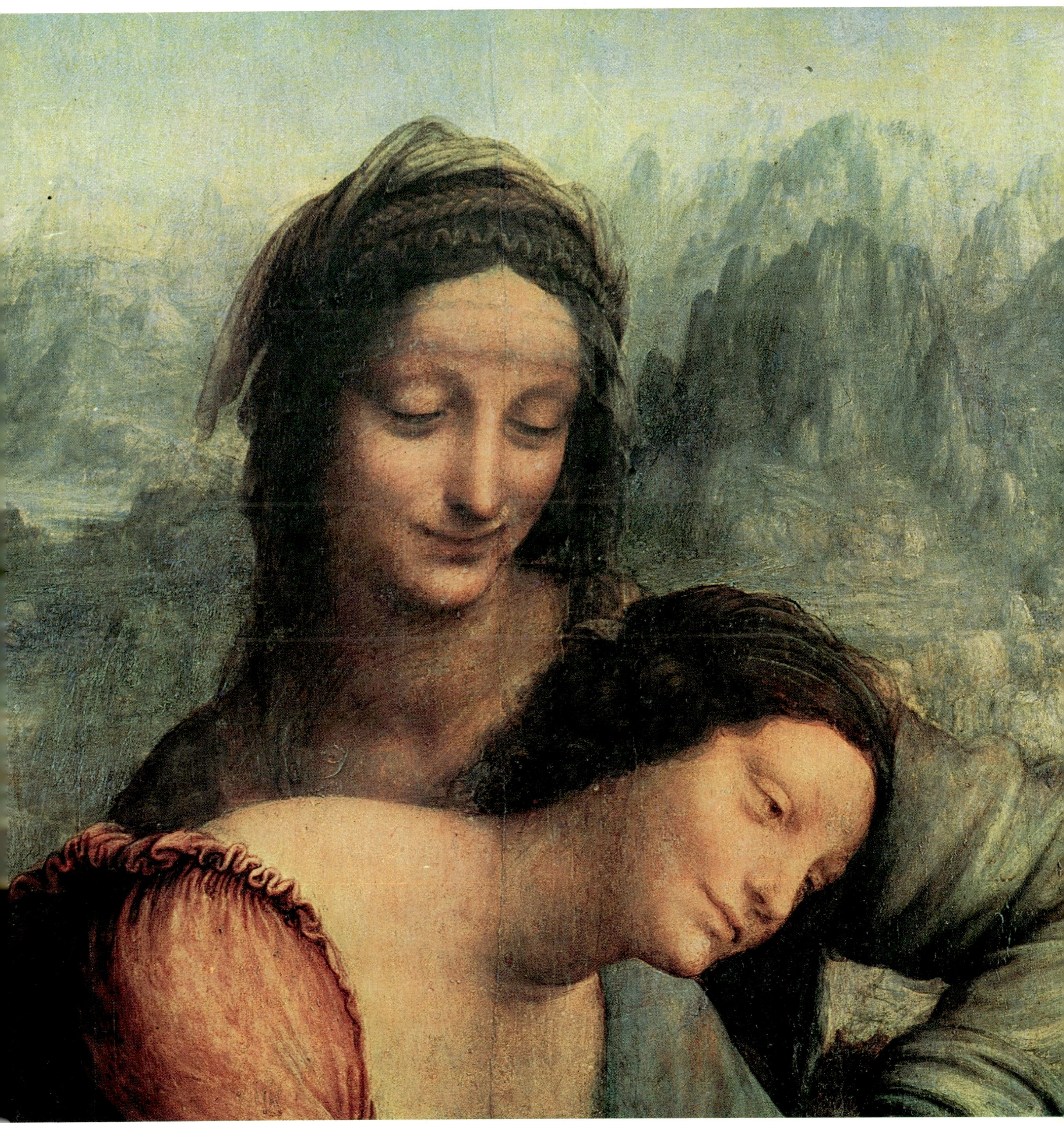

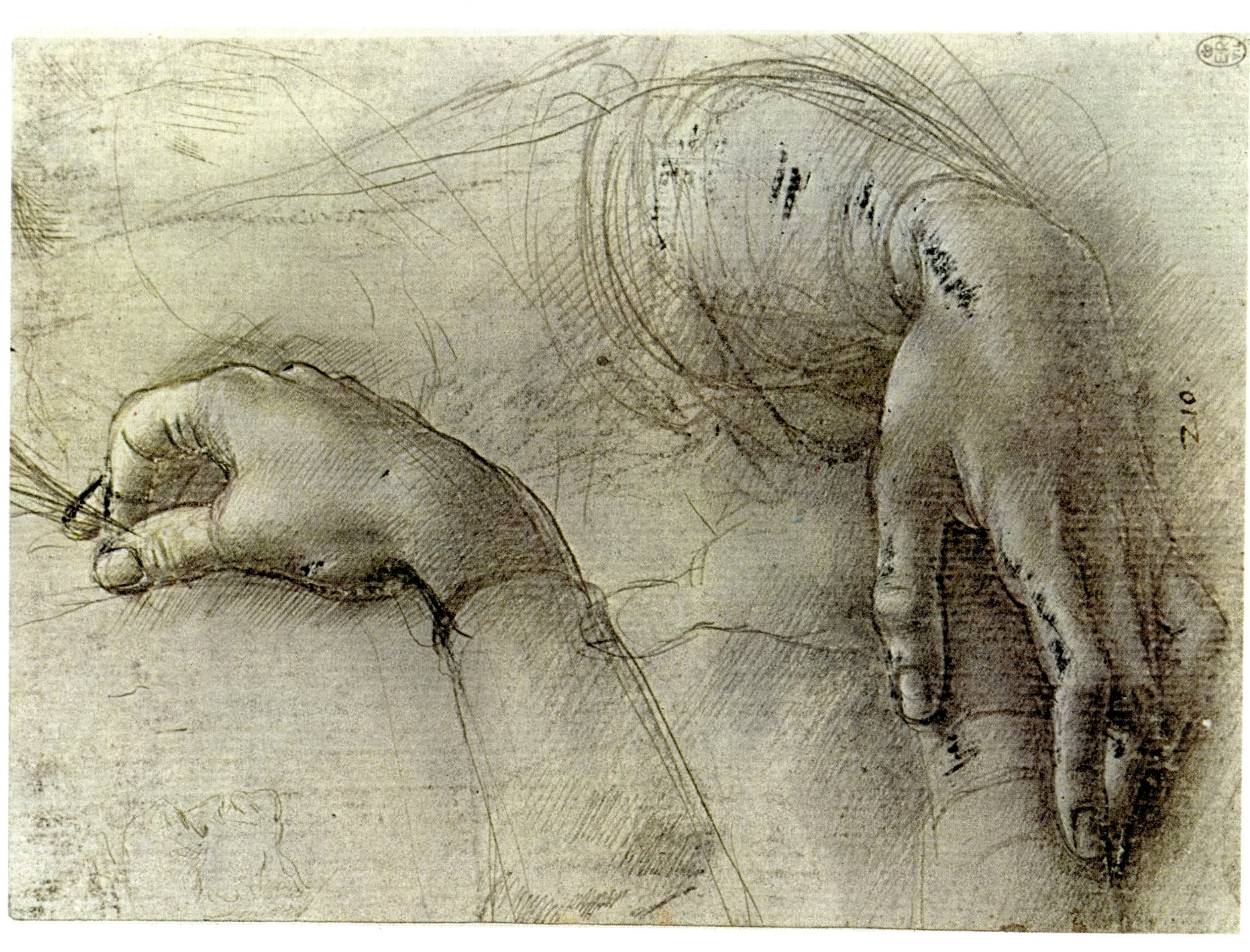

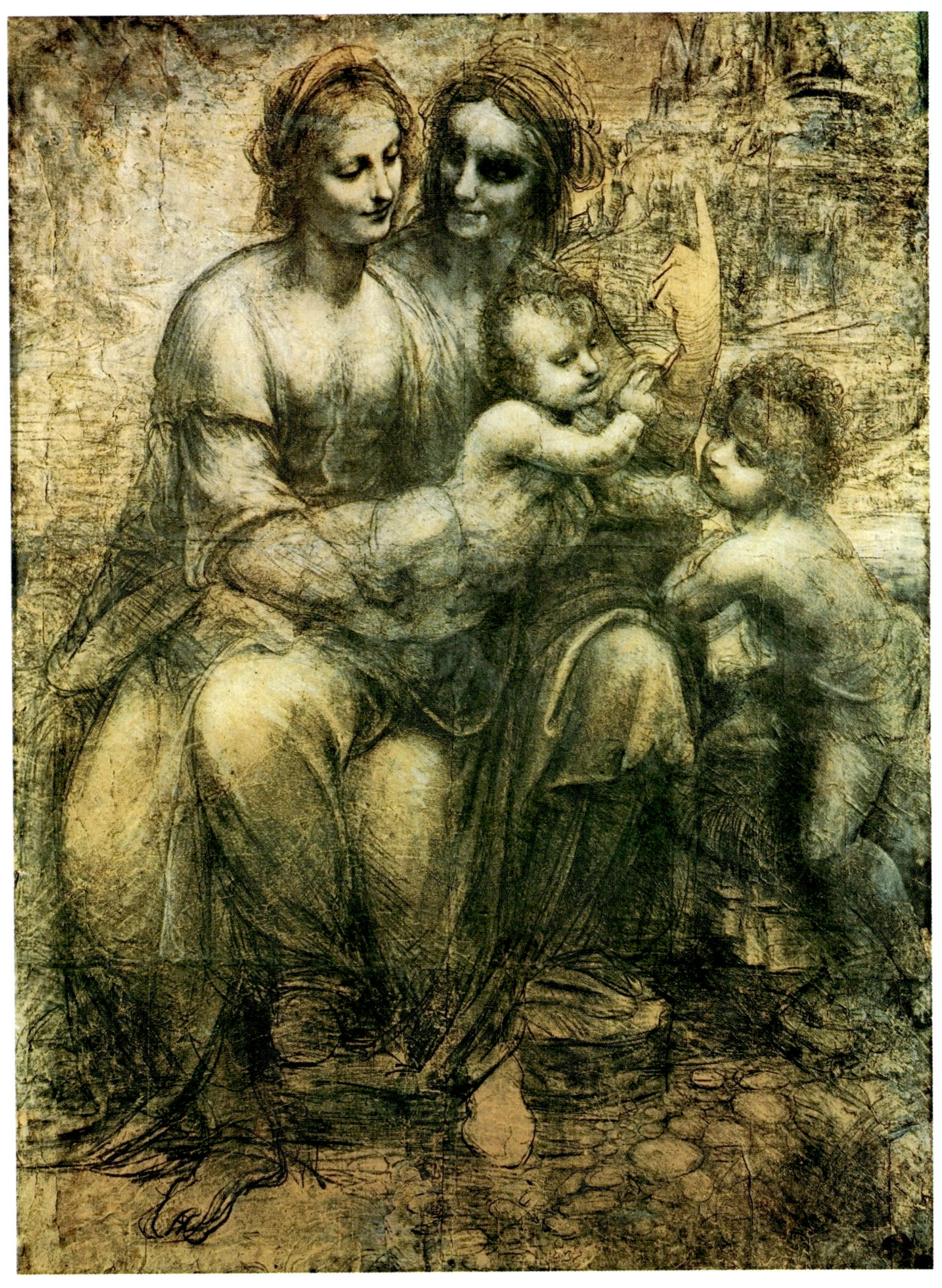

XXIII

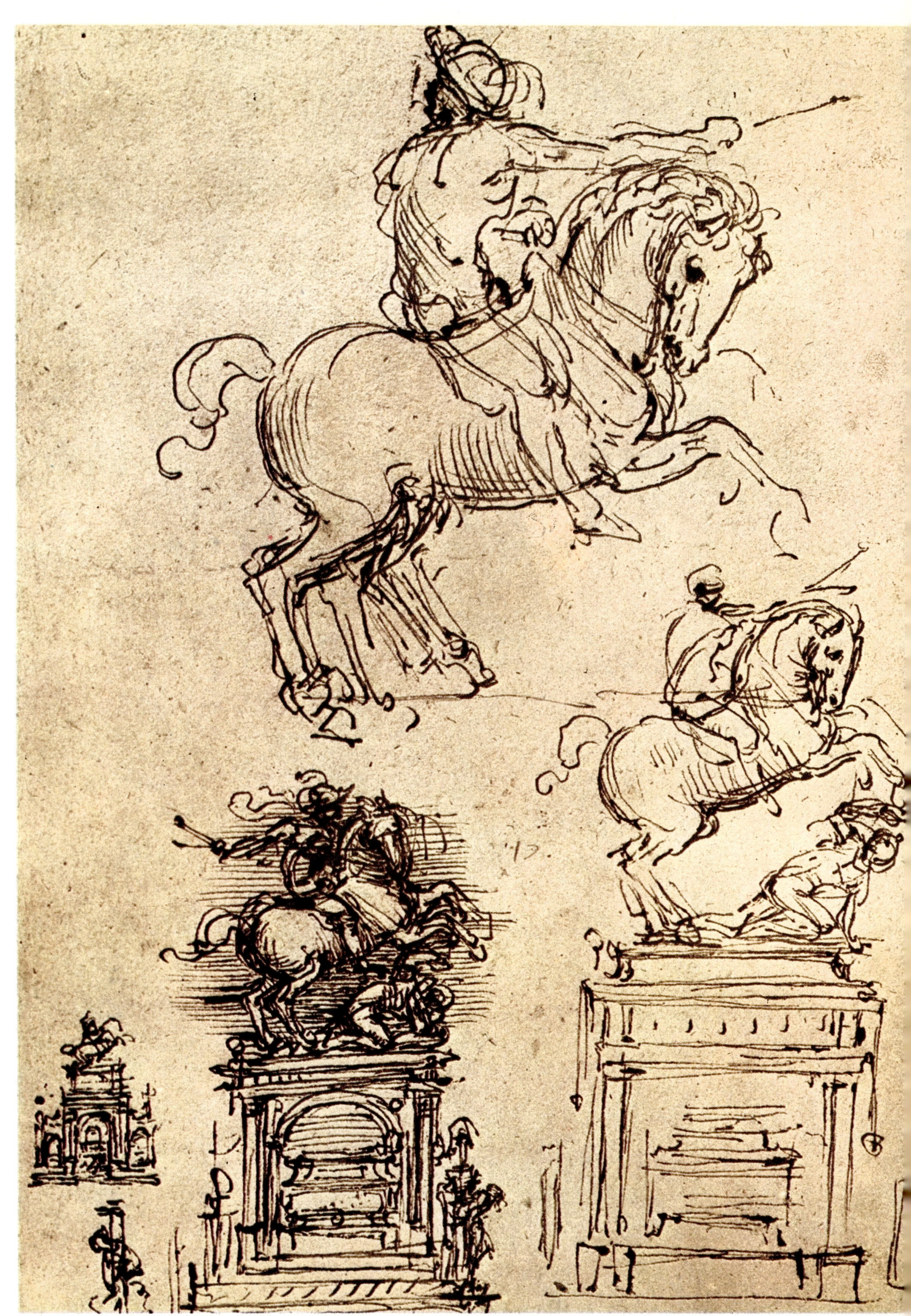

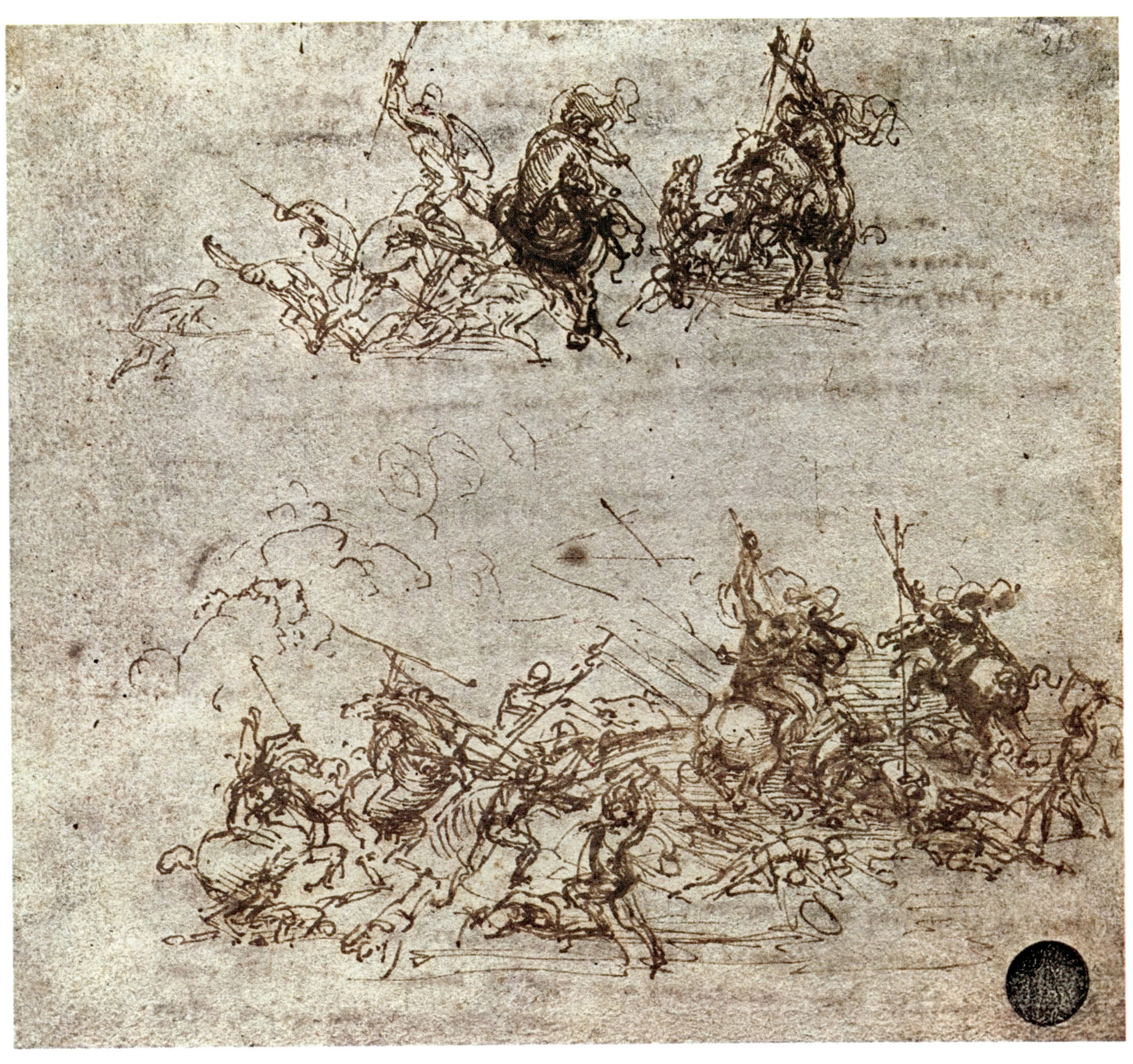

XXV

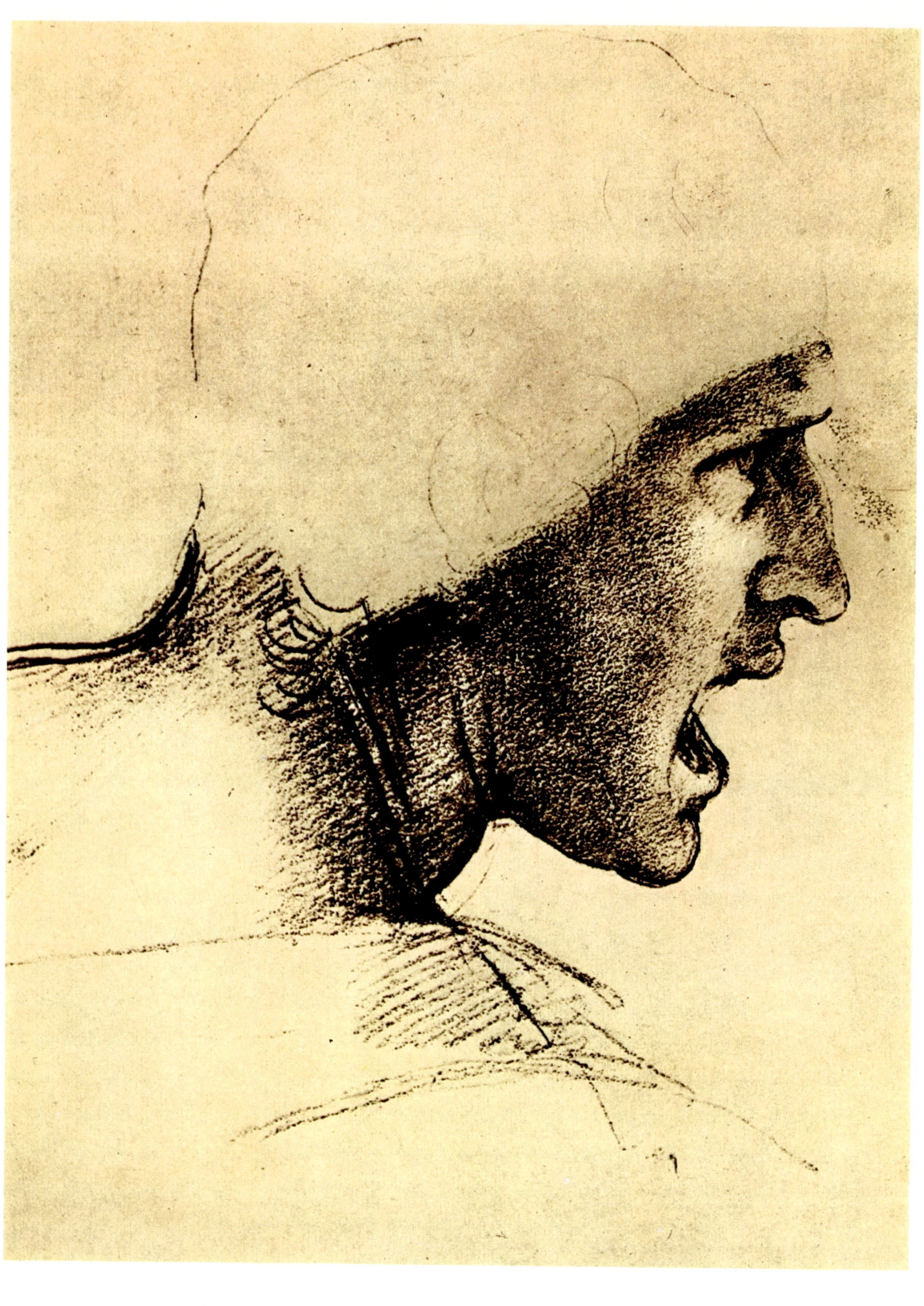

XXVI

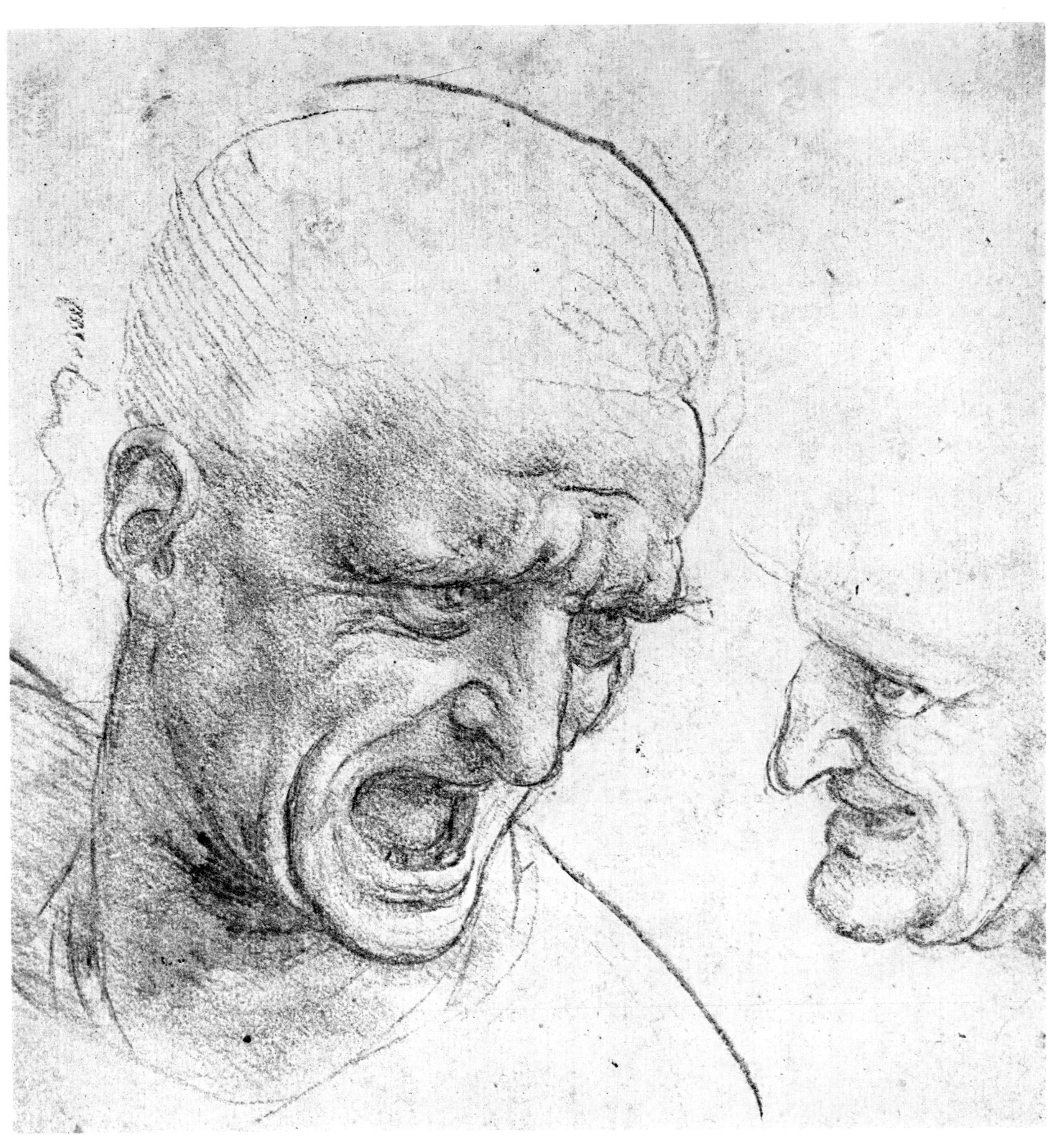

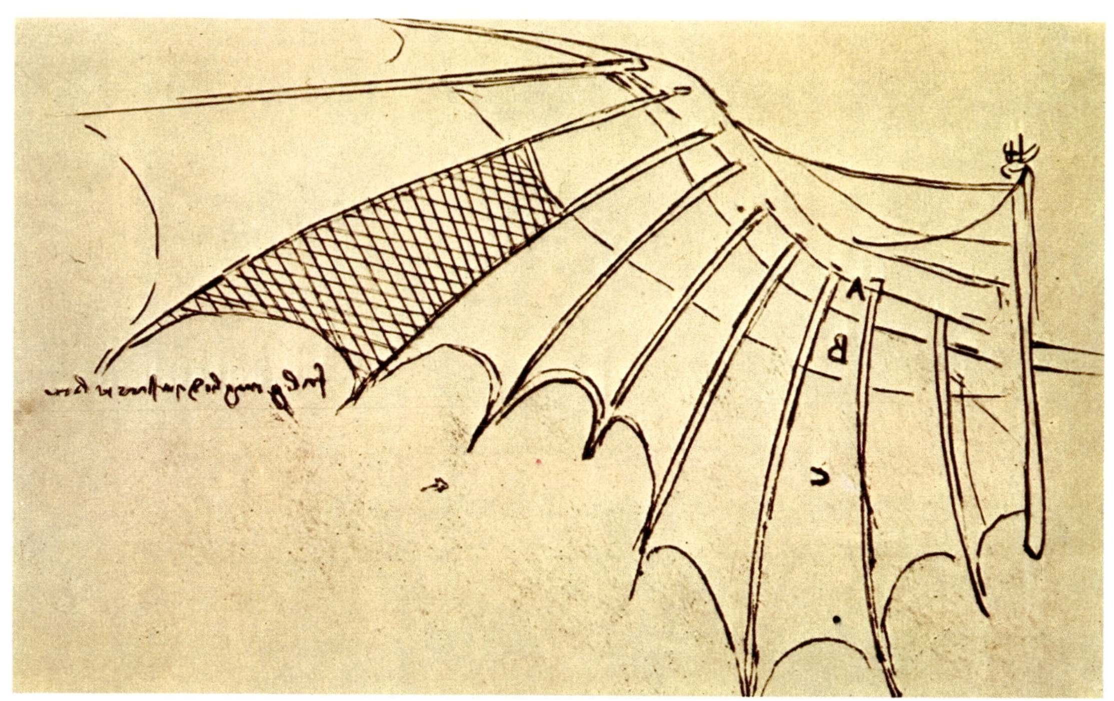
A
B

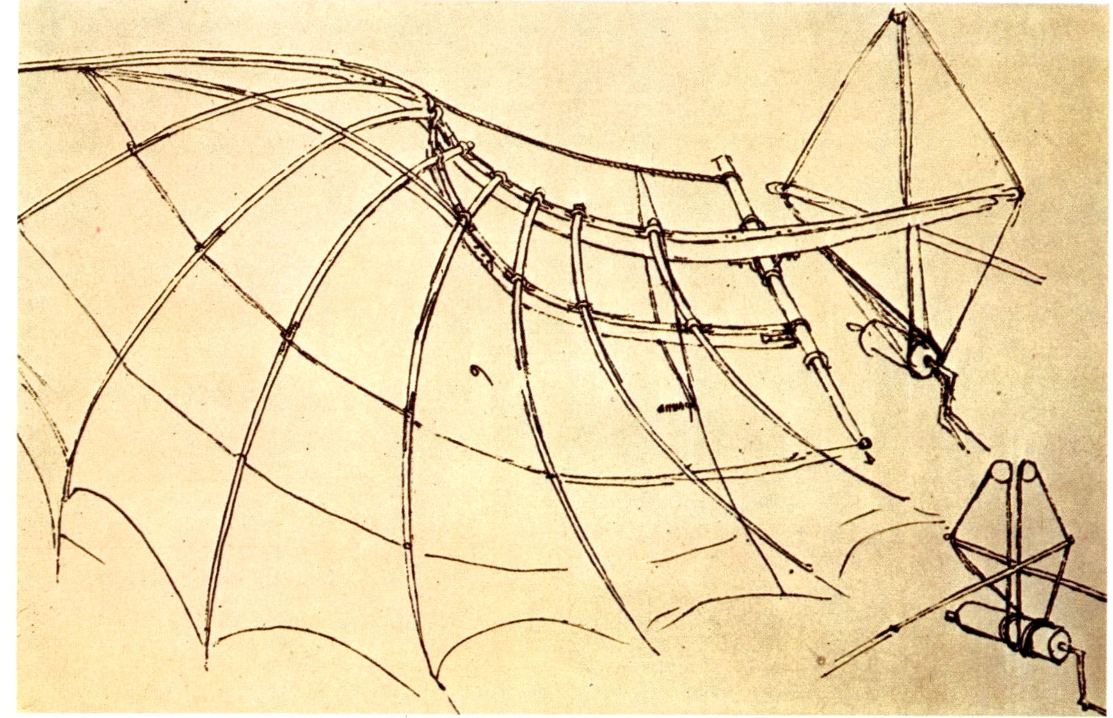

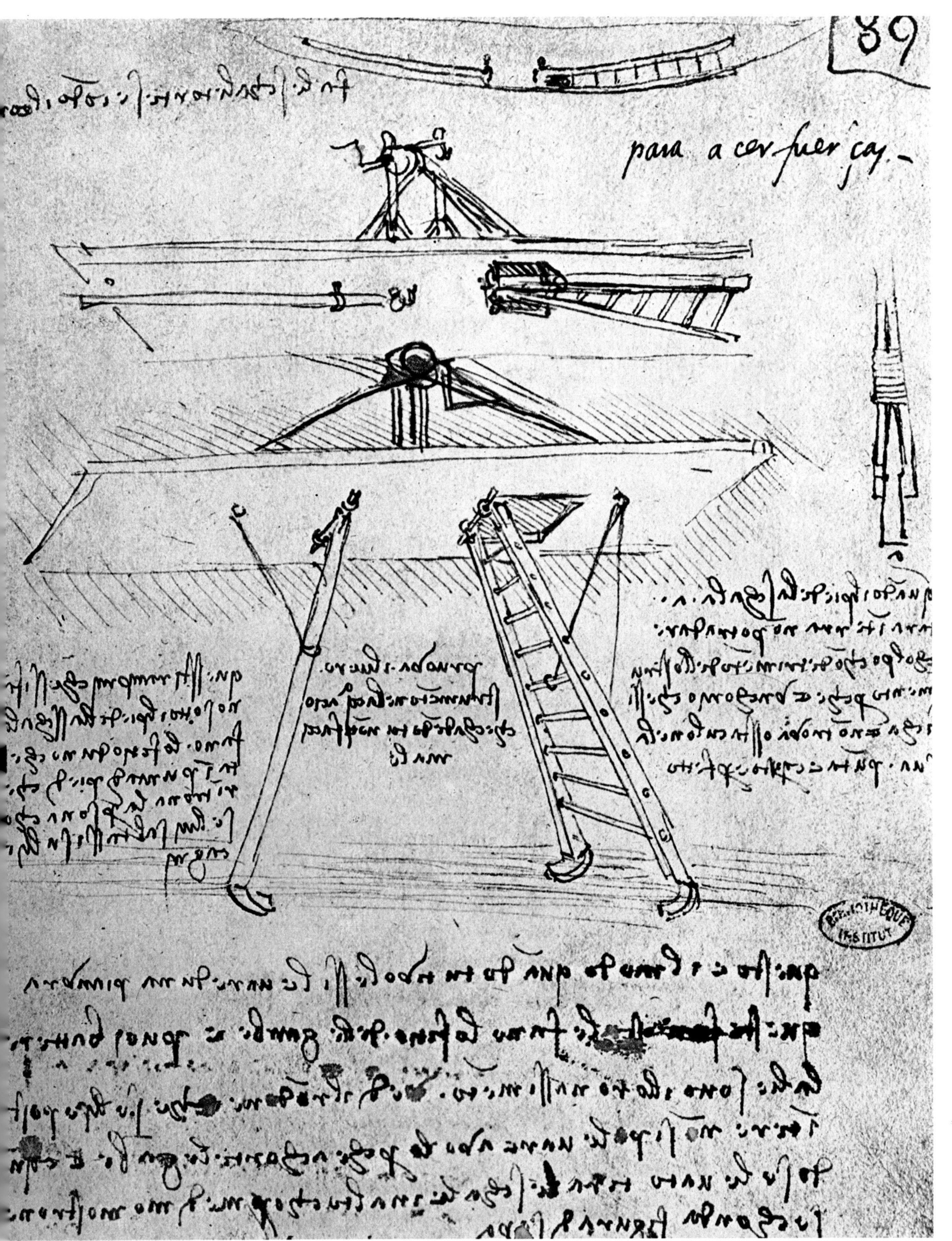
89
para a cer. fuer çay.-
BIBLIOTHEQUE INSTITUT

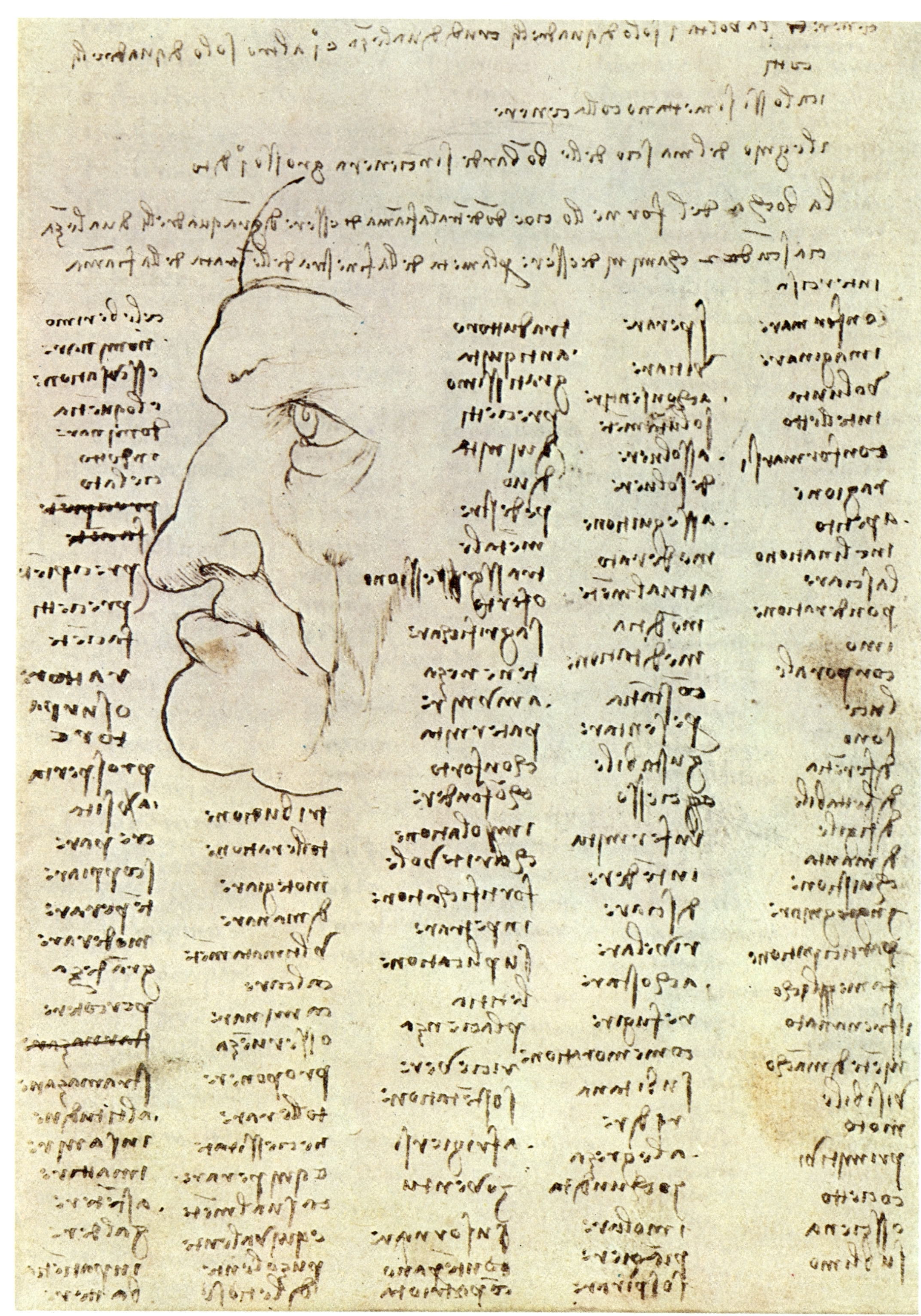

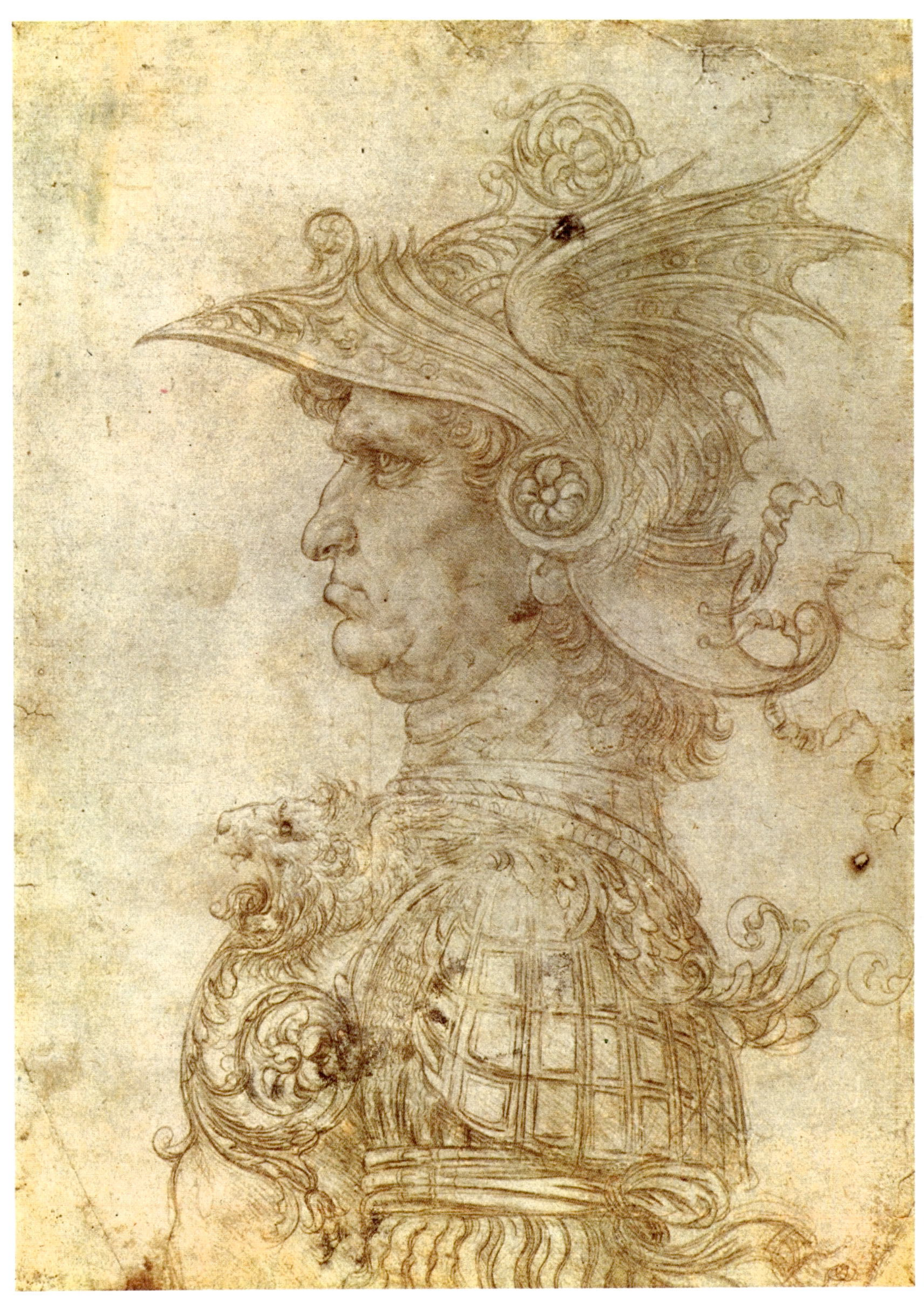

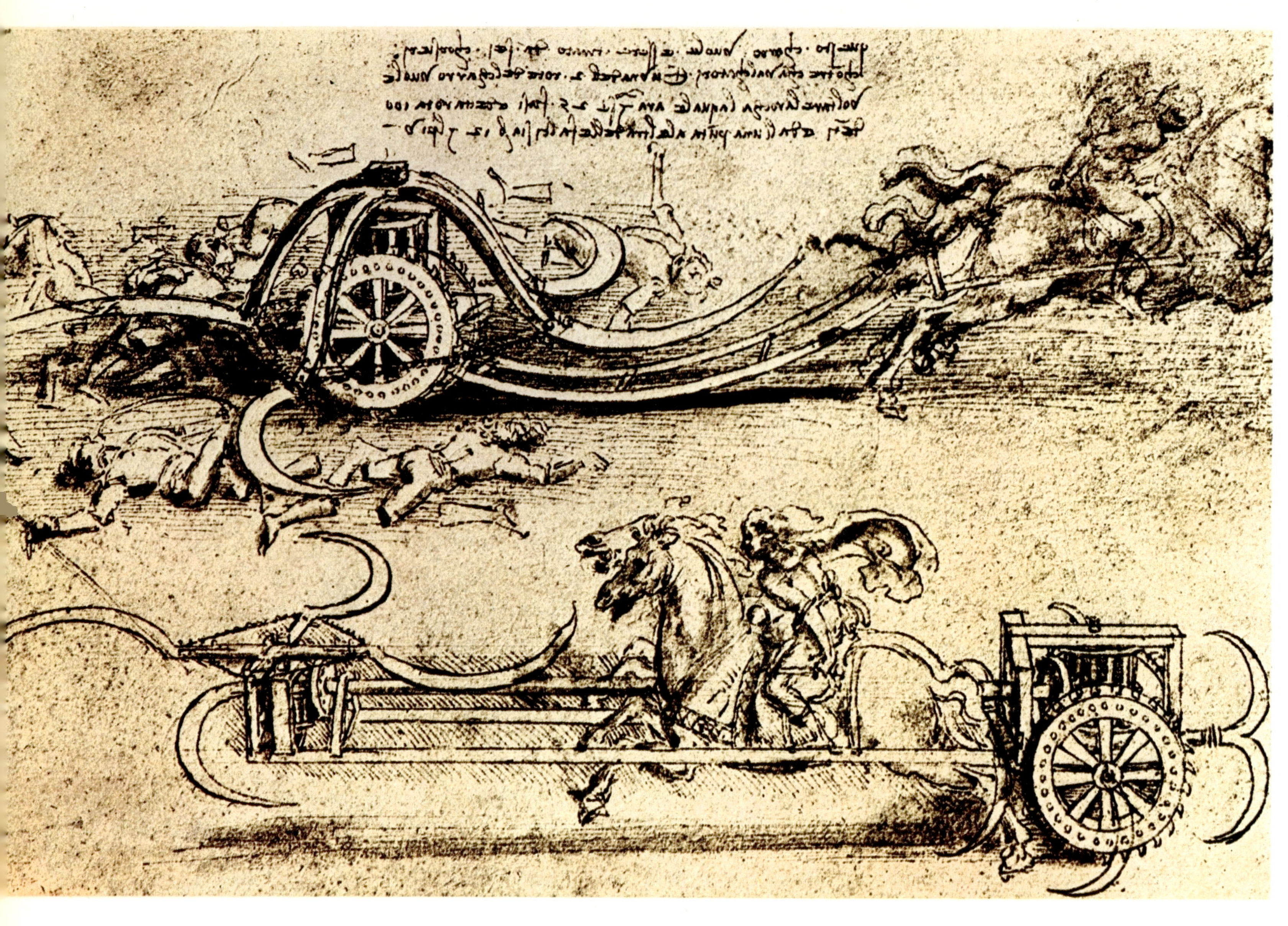

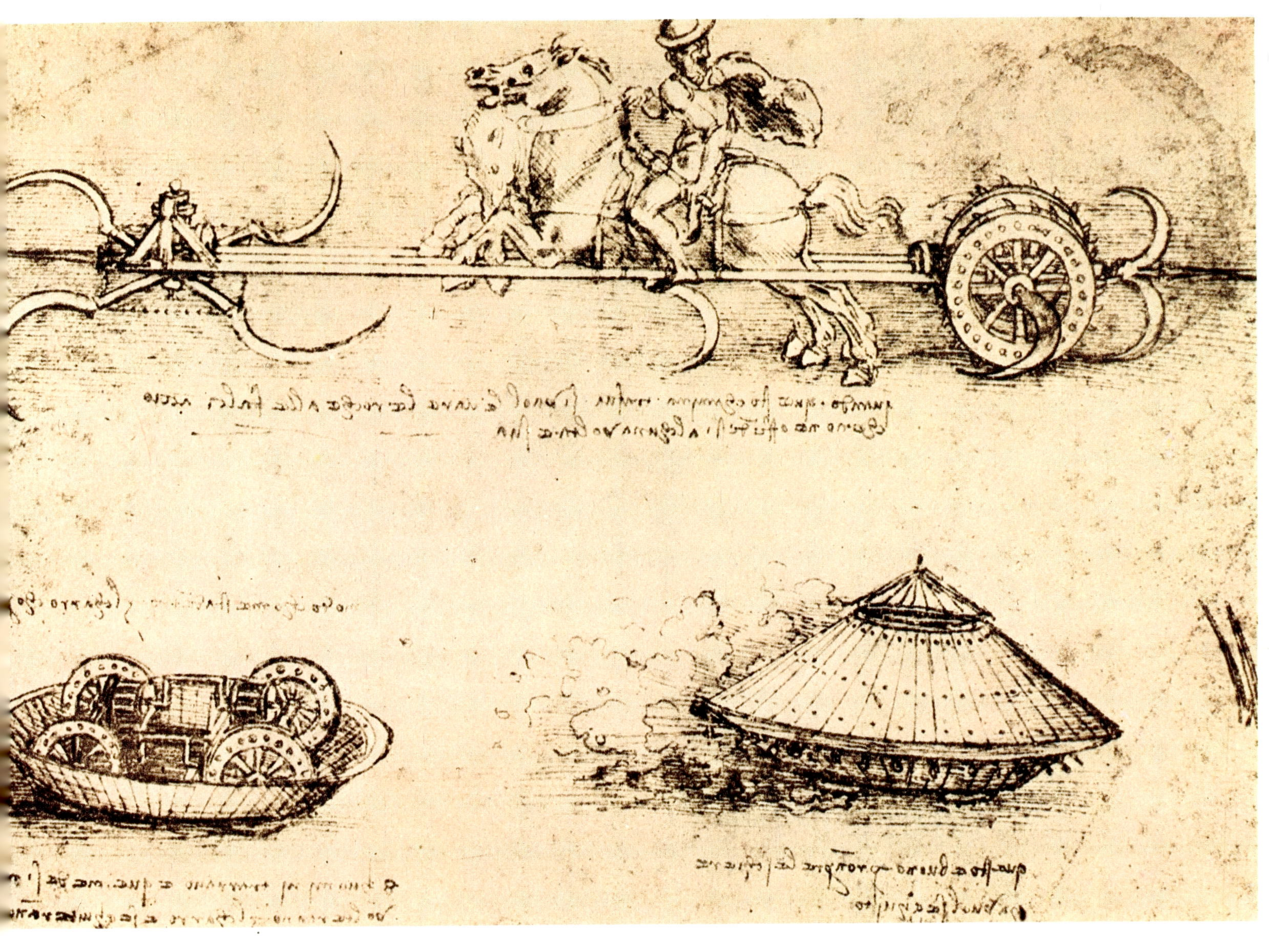

XXXIII

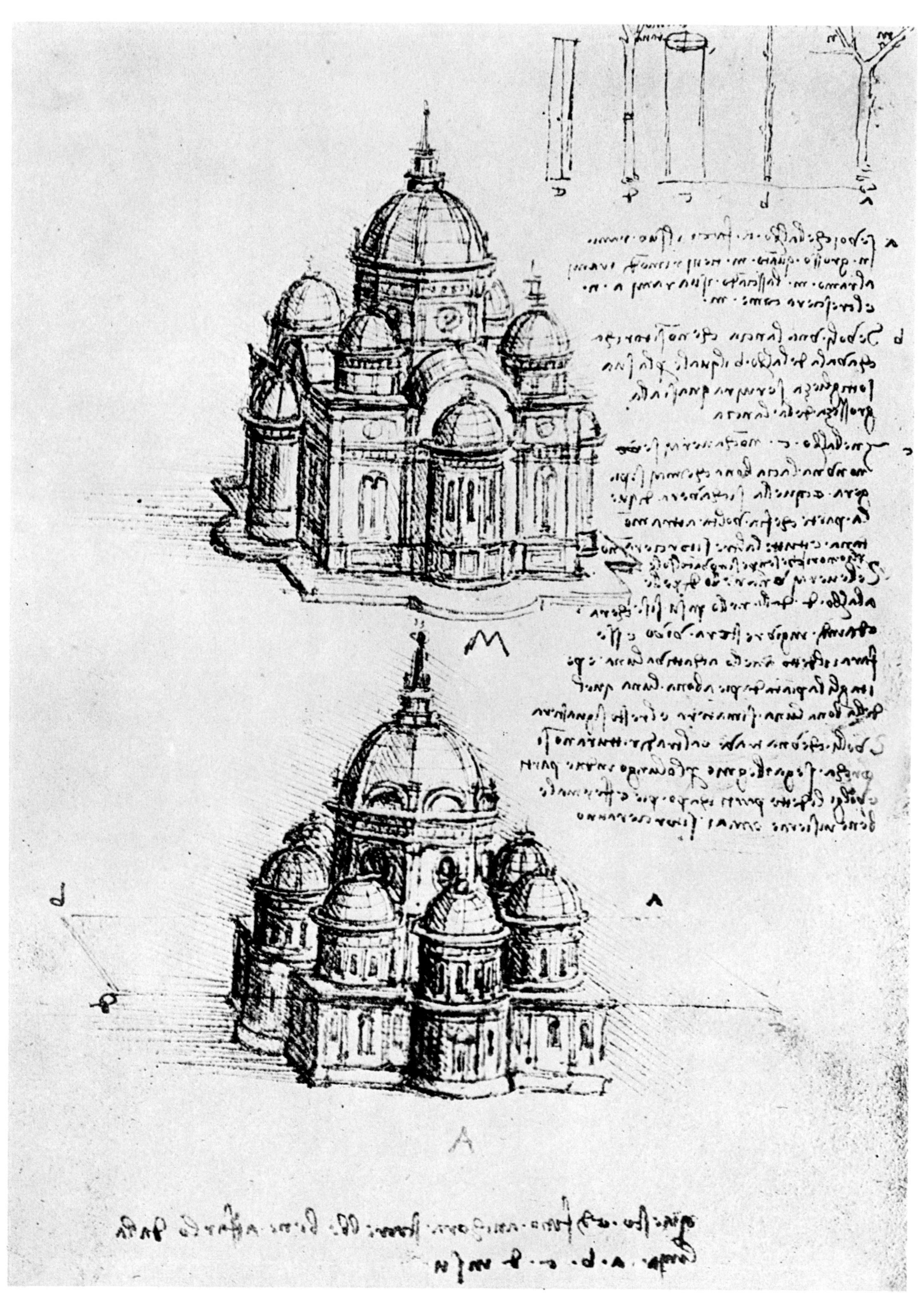
A

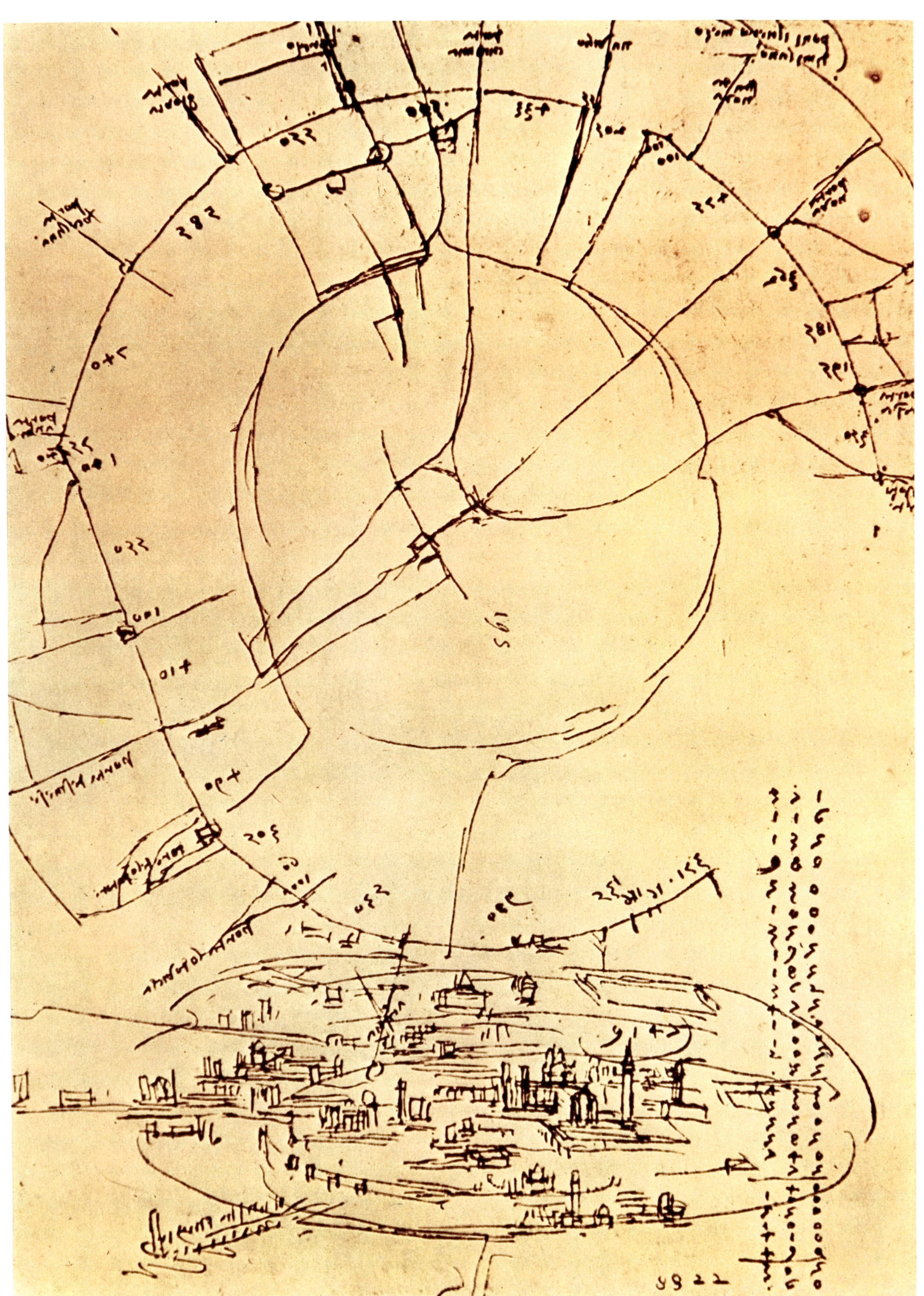

XXXV

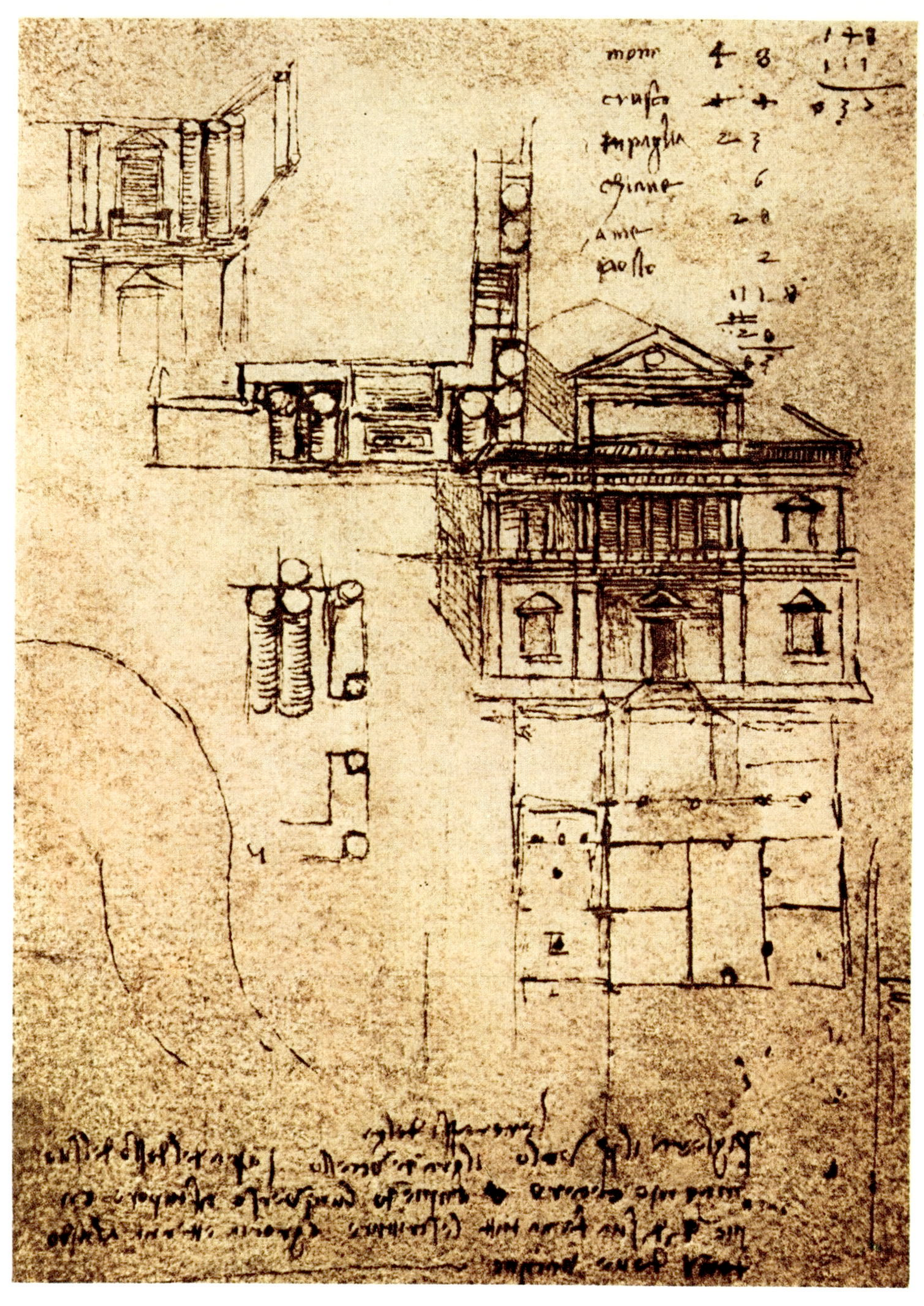

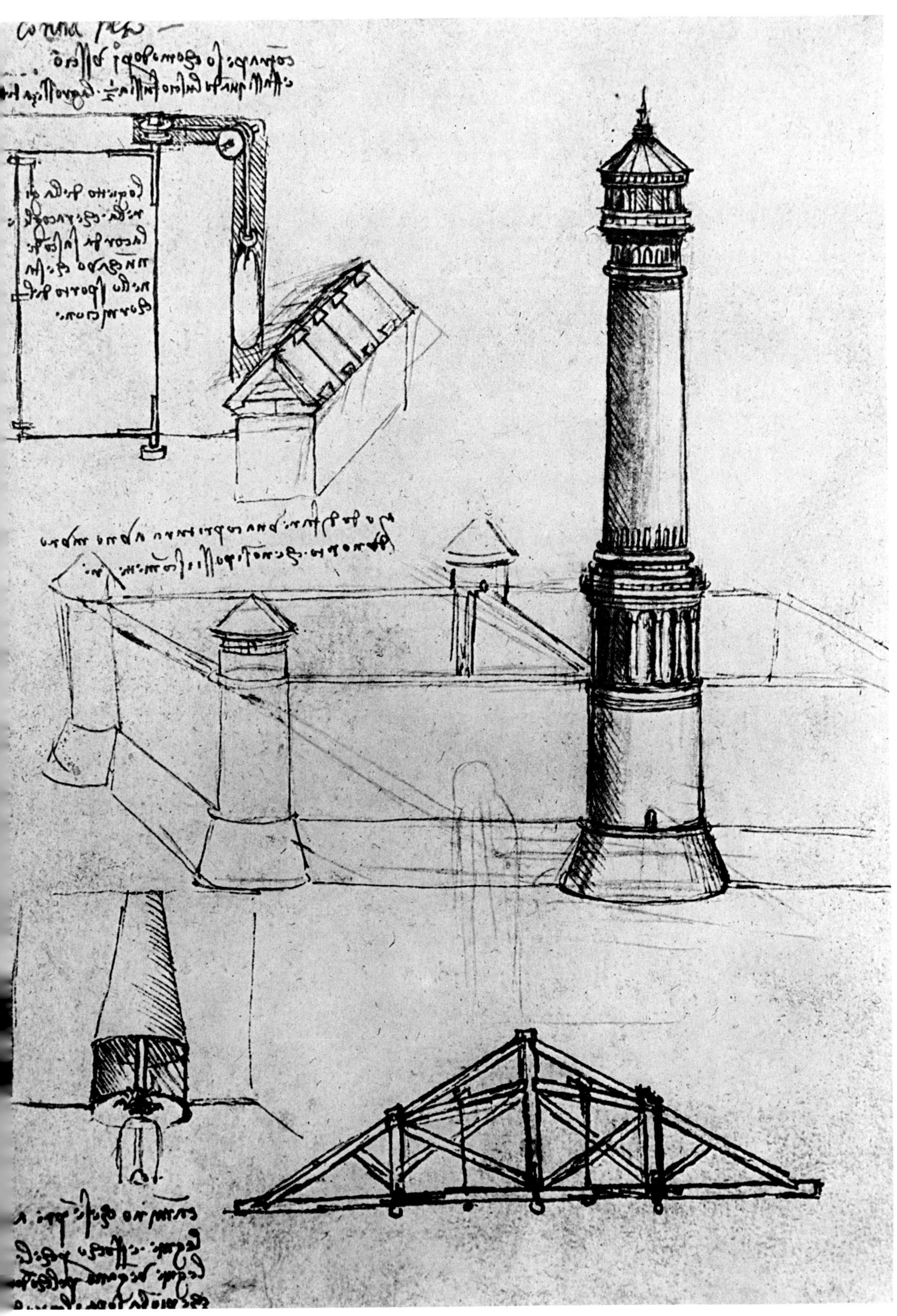

XXXVII

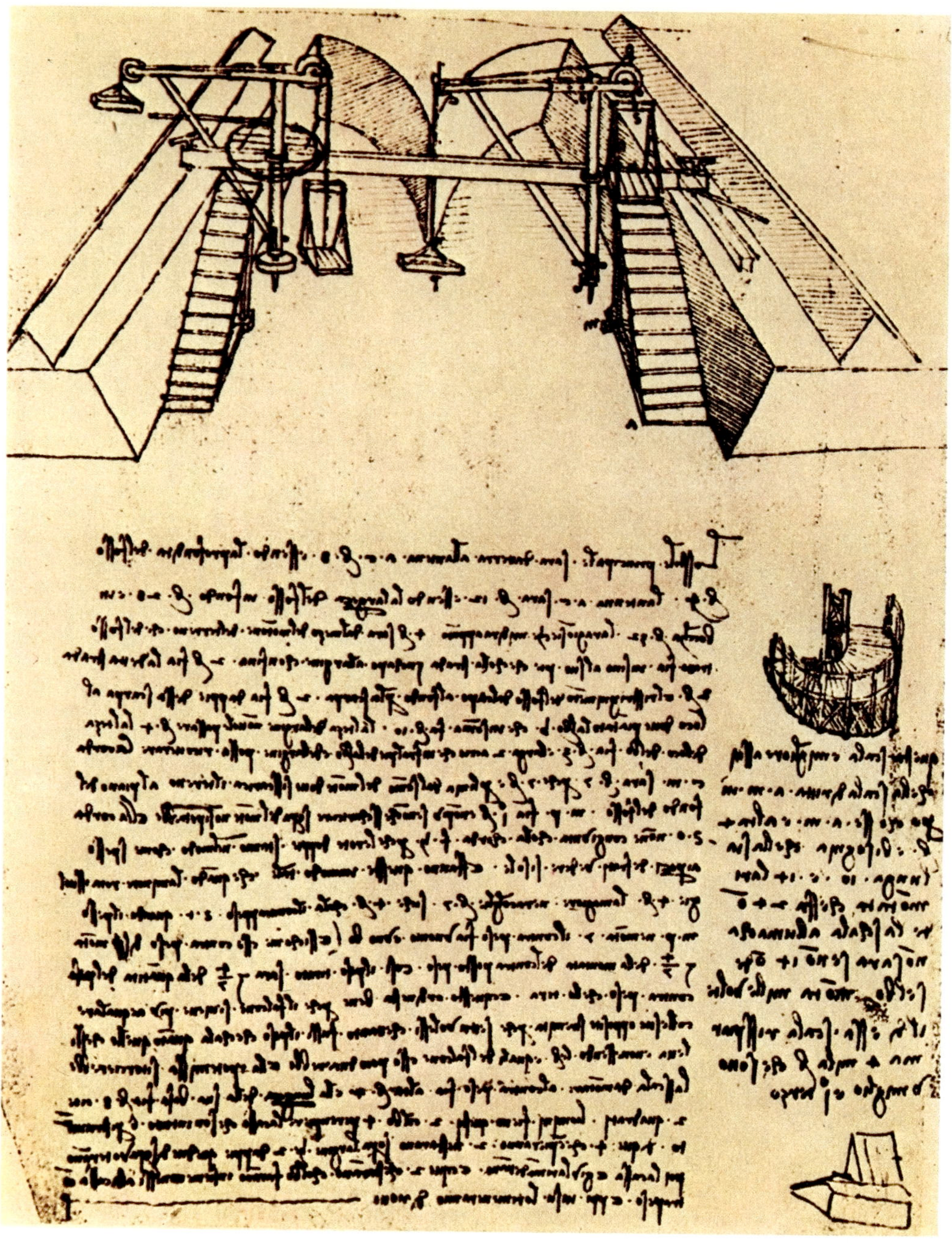

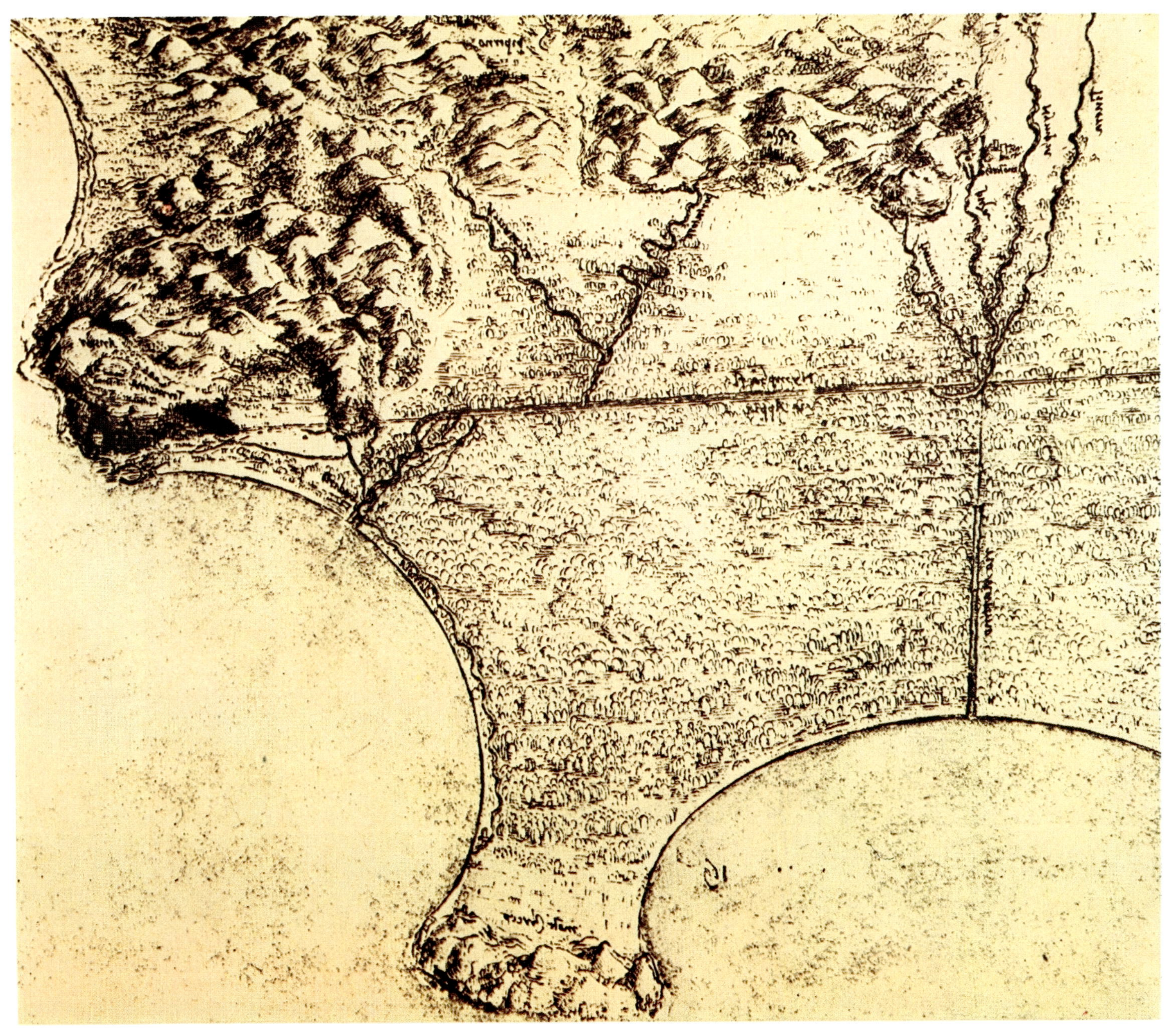

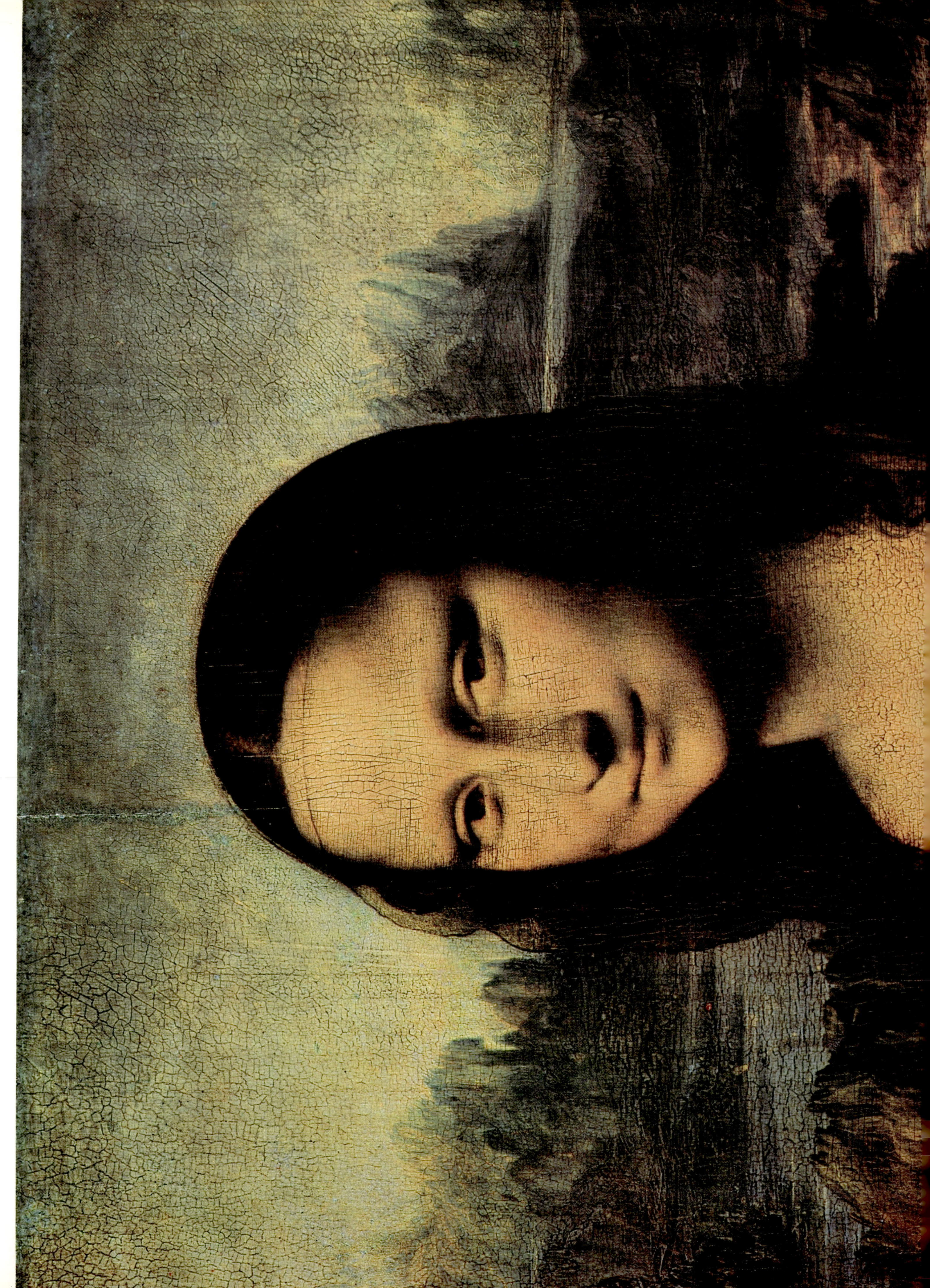

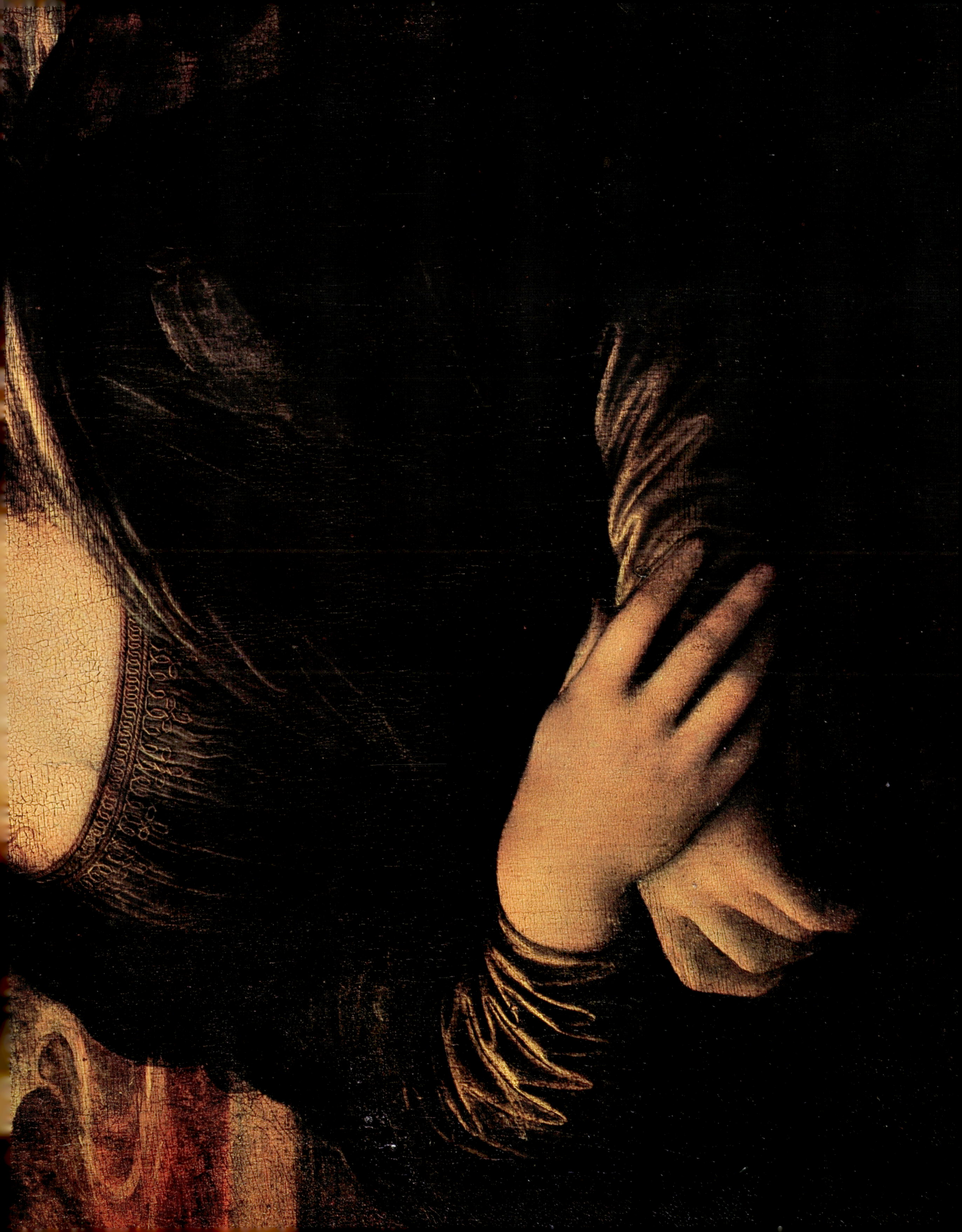

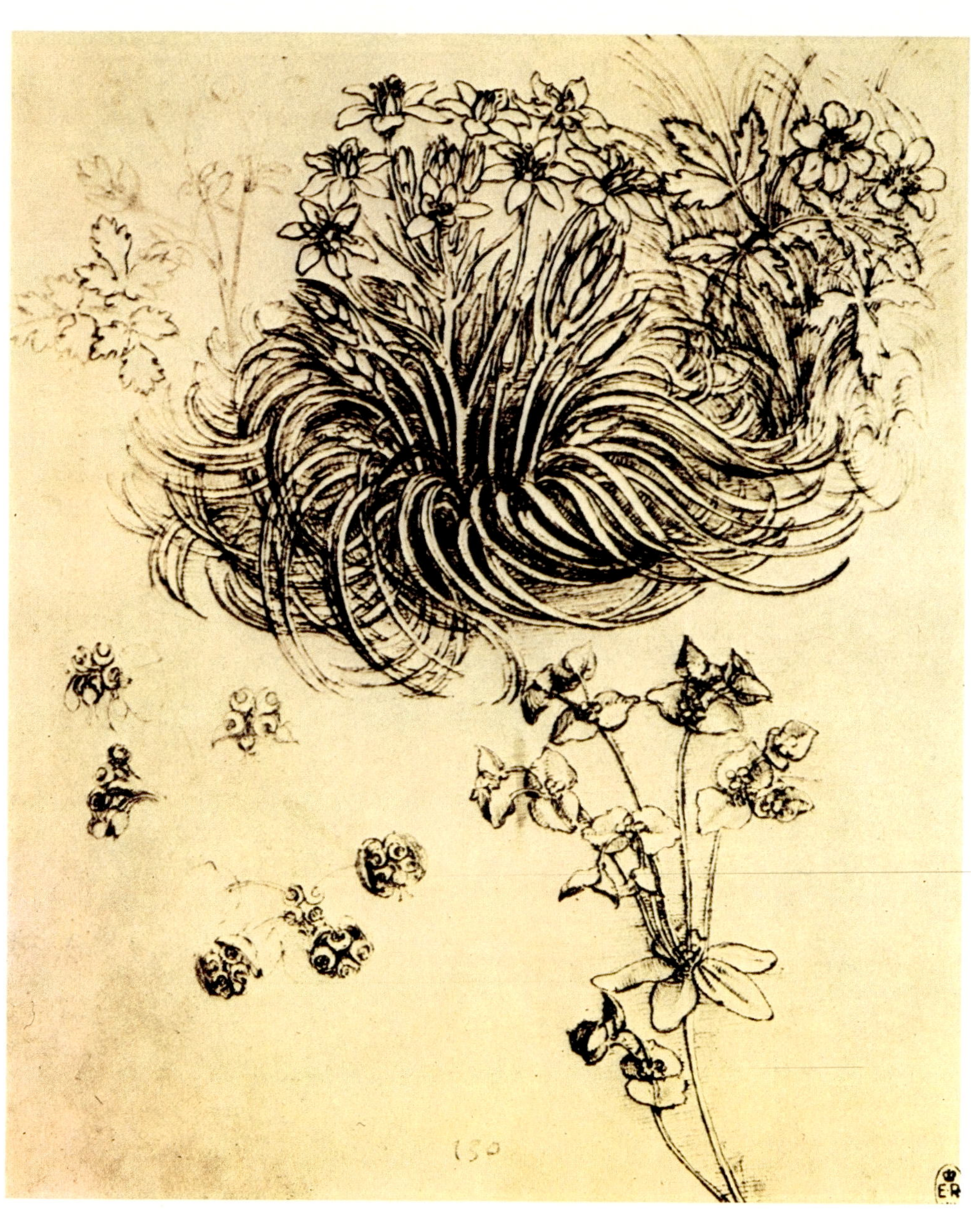

XLII

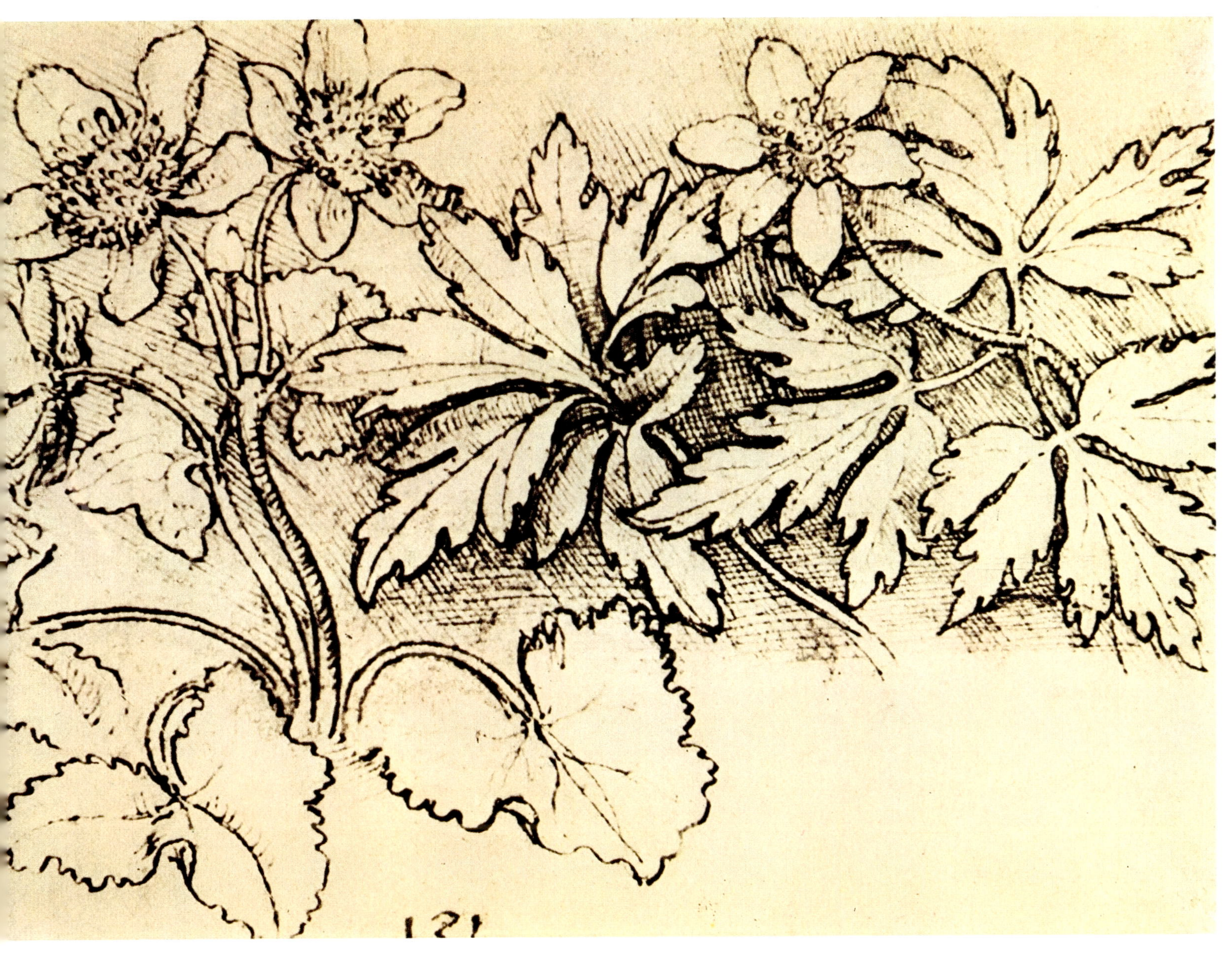

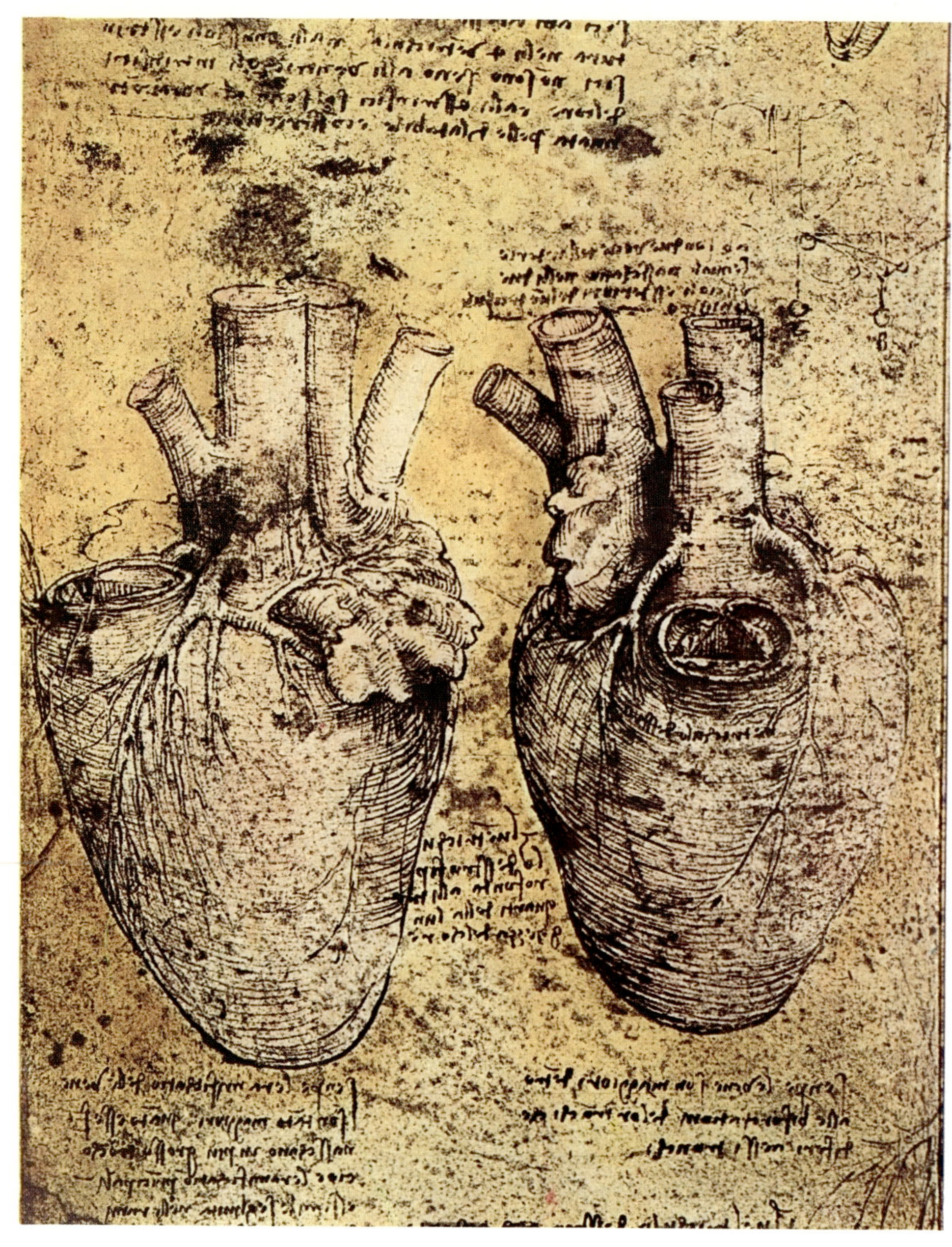

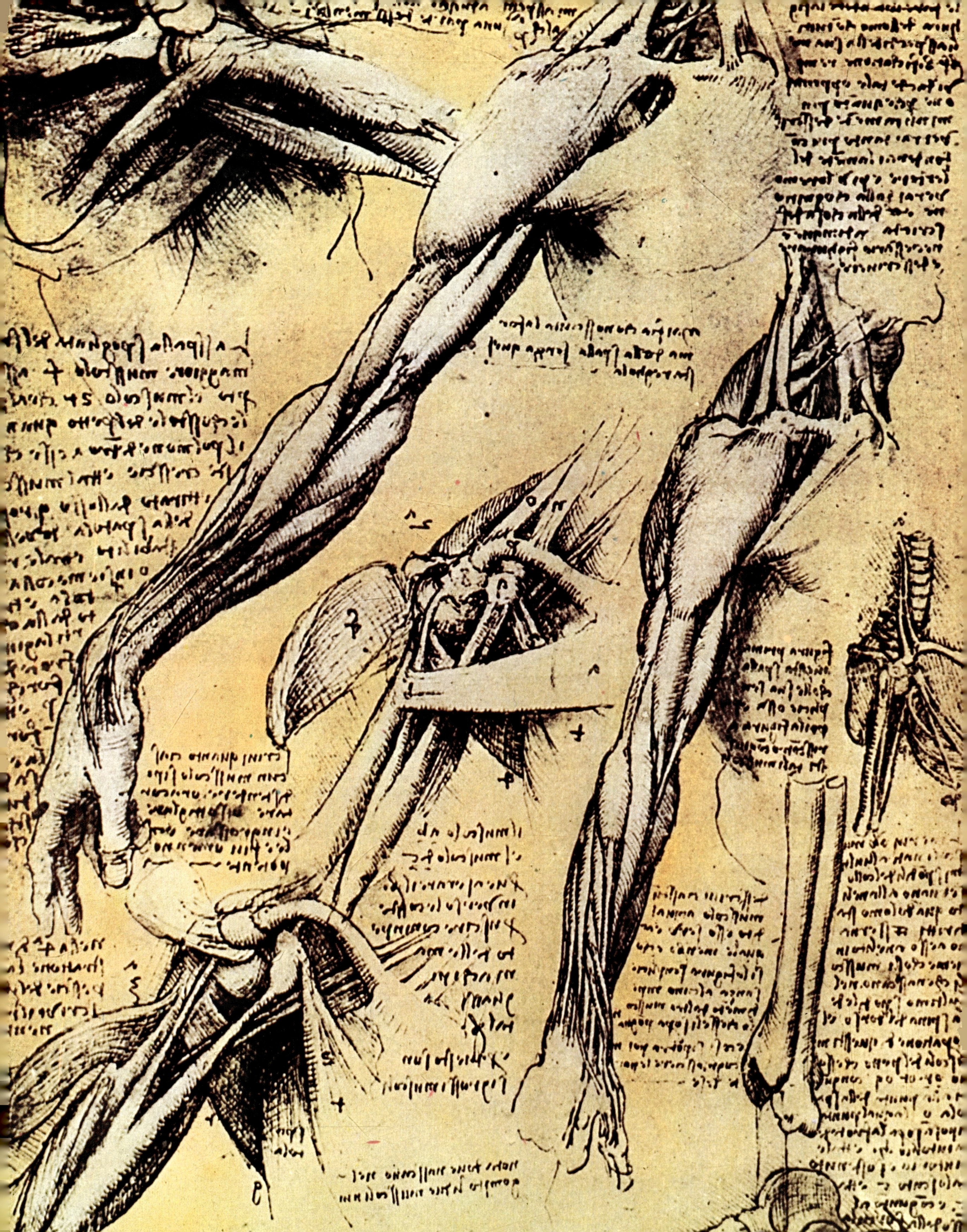

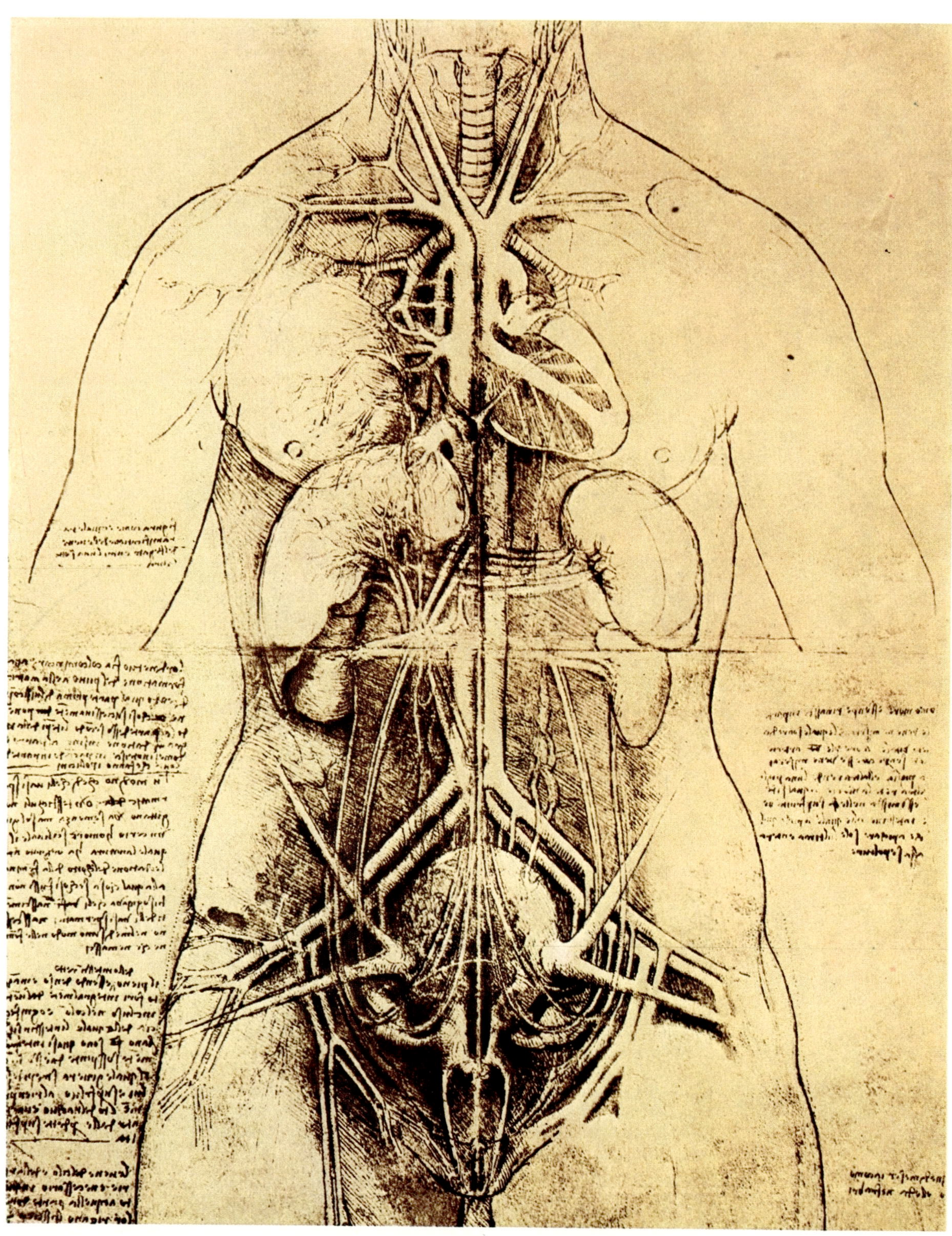

XLVI

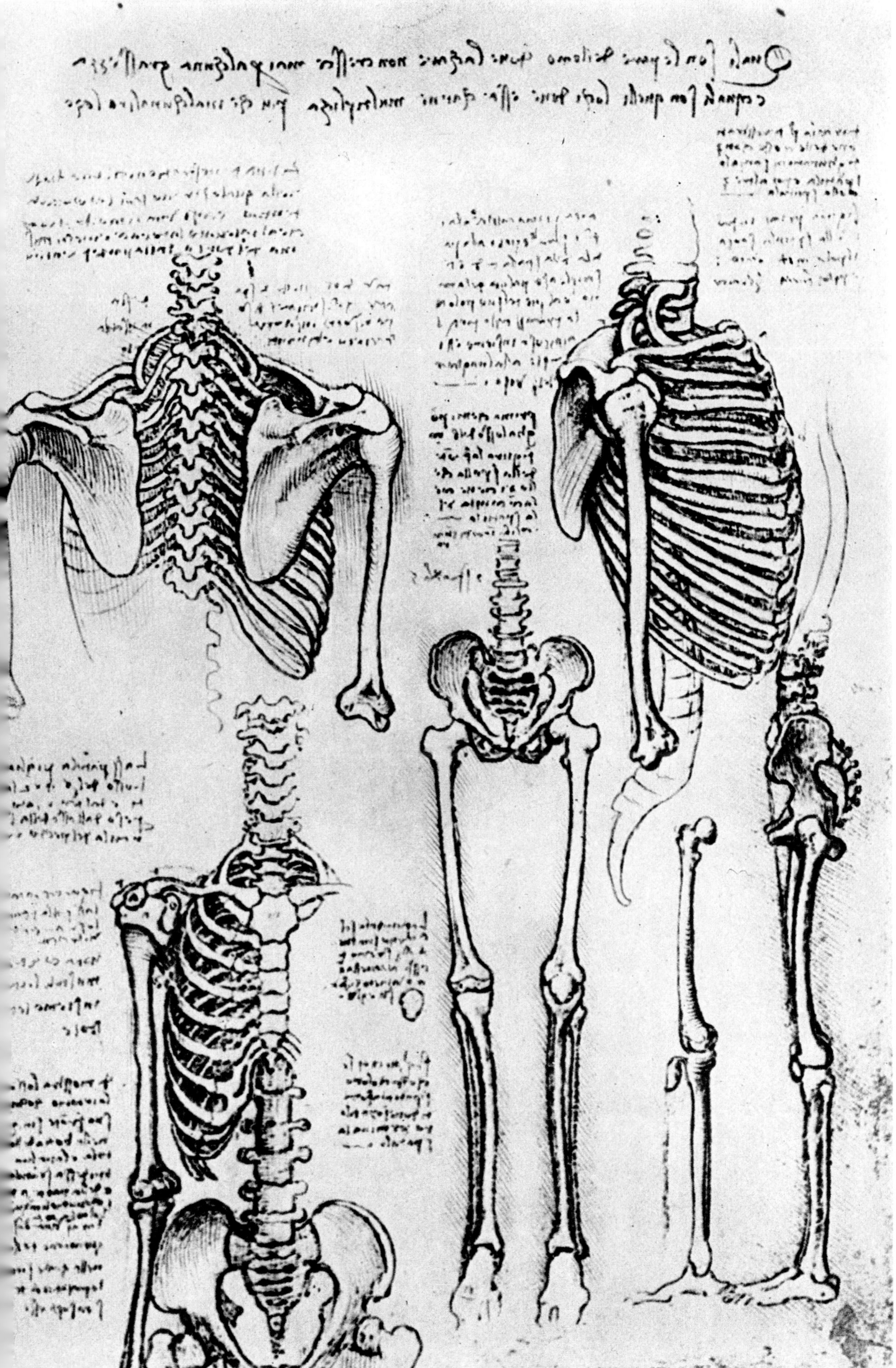

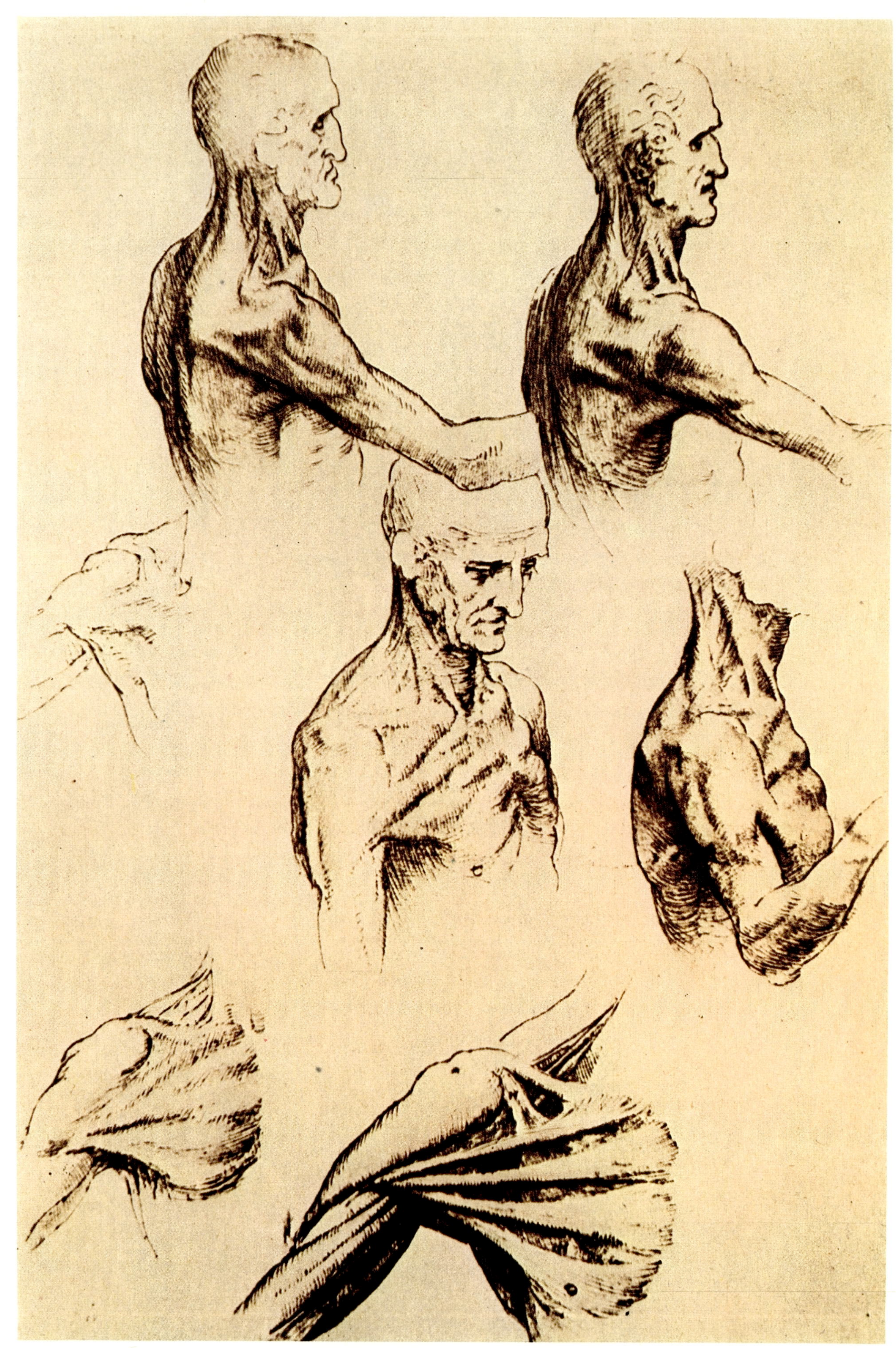

XLVIII

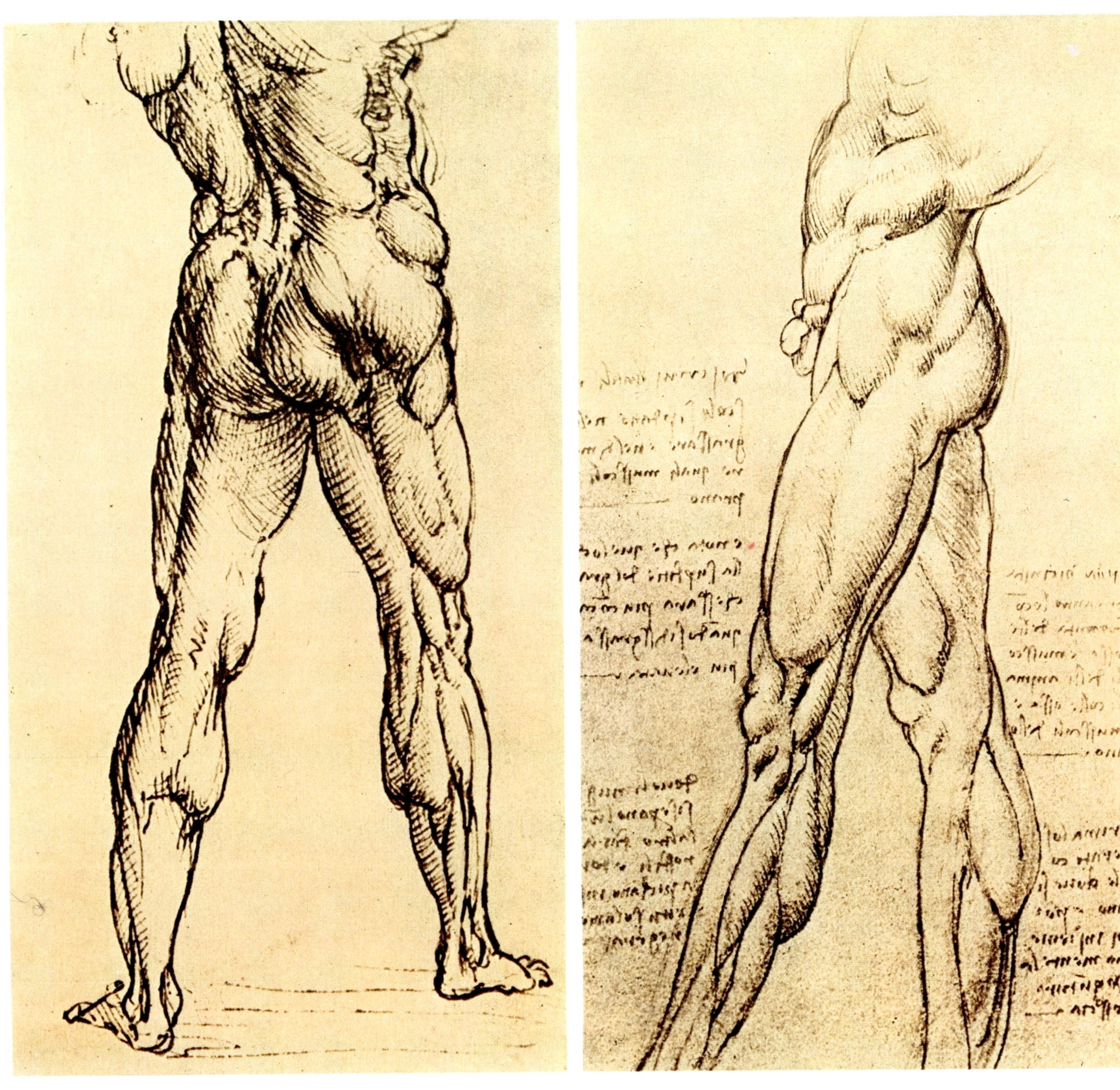

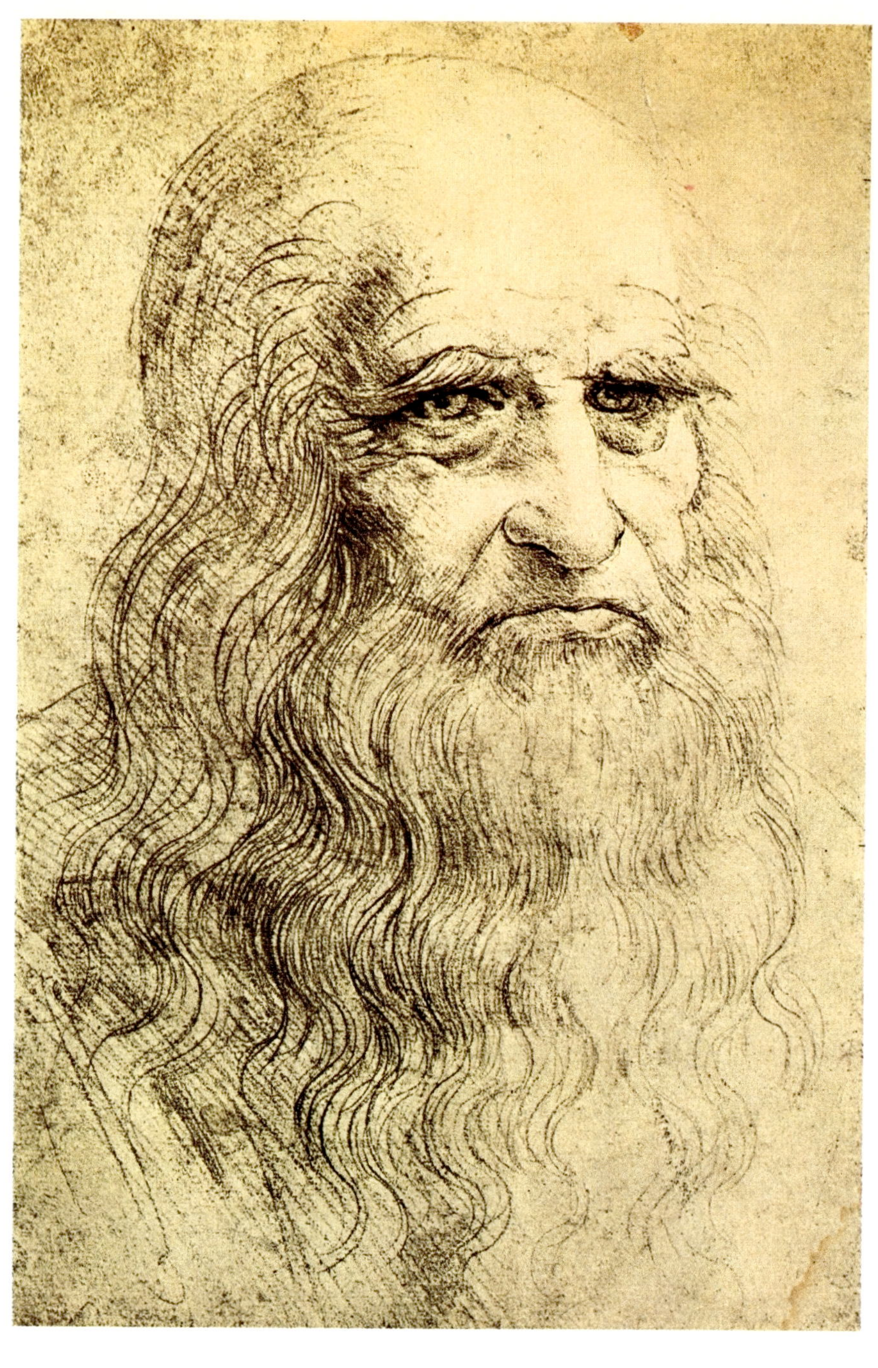

L

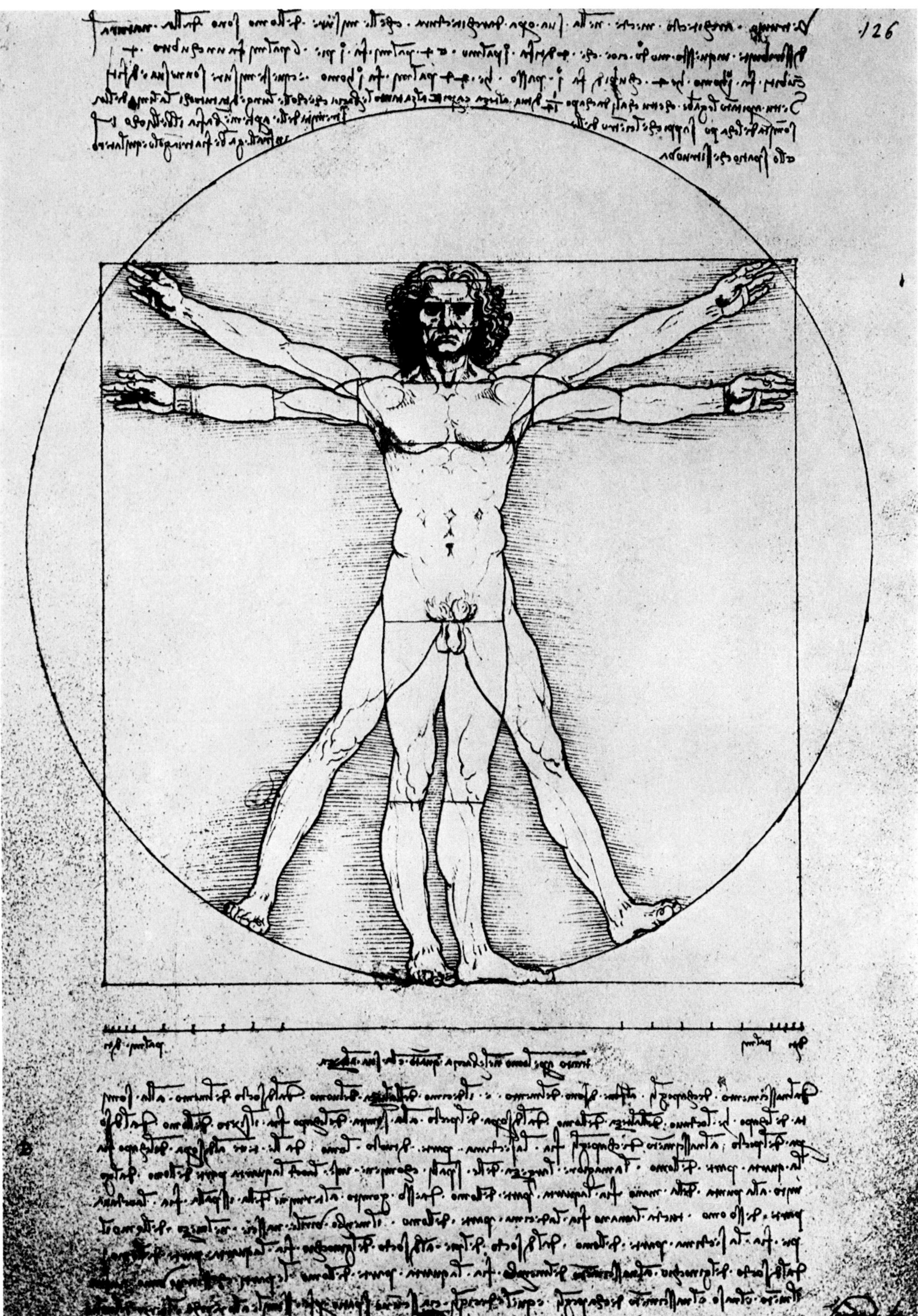
126

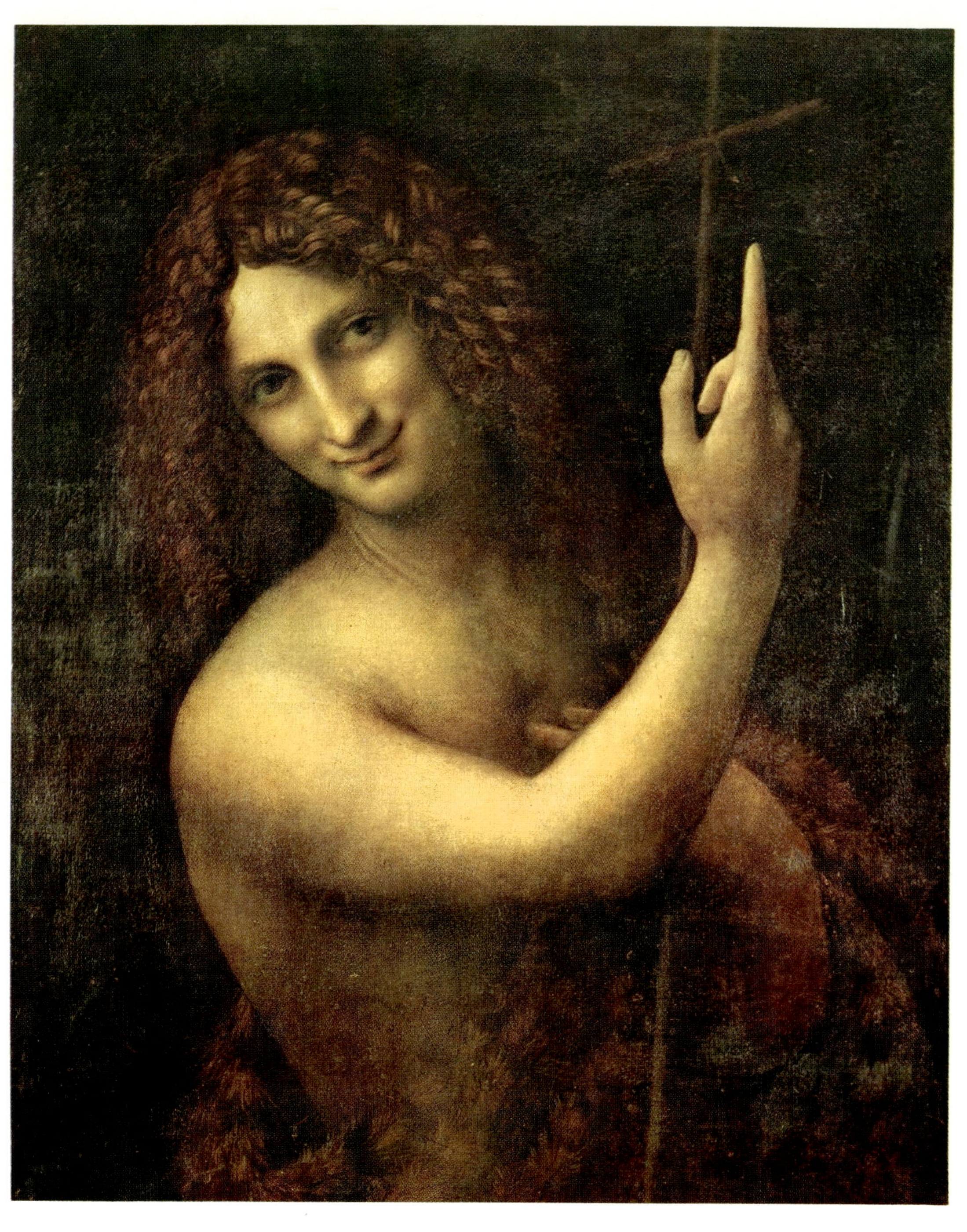

LII

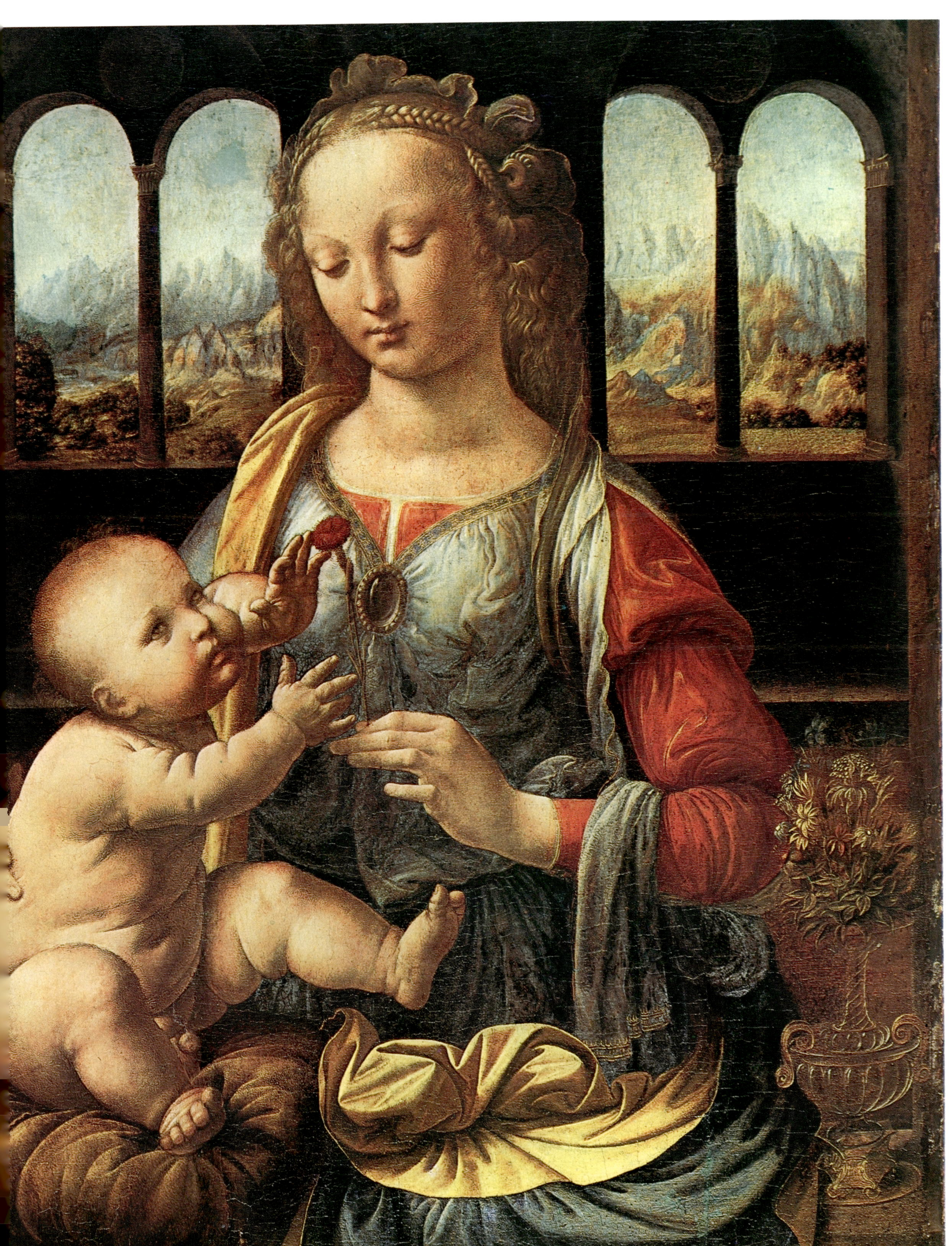

LIII

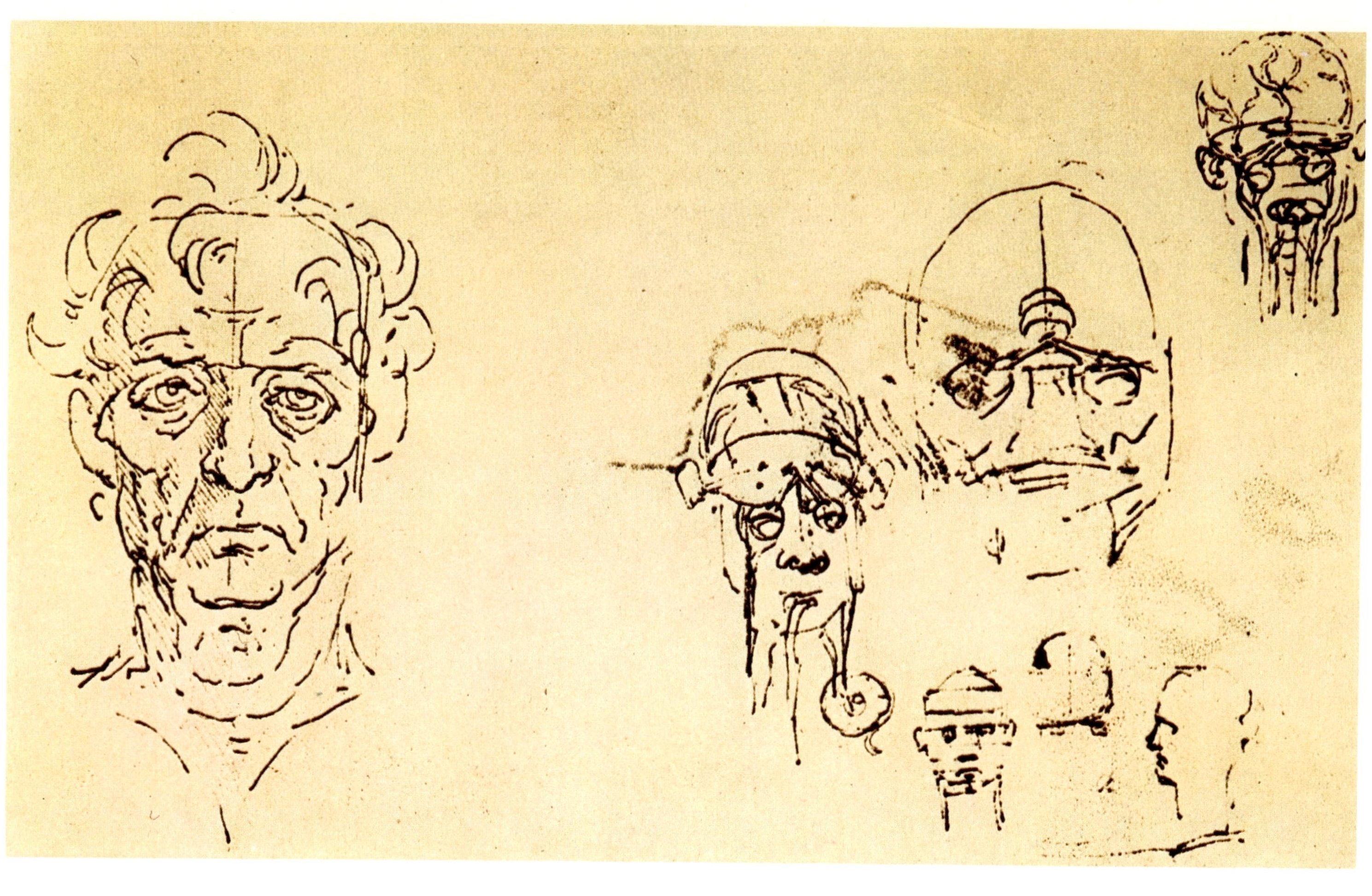

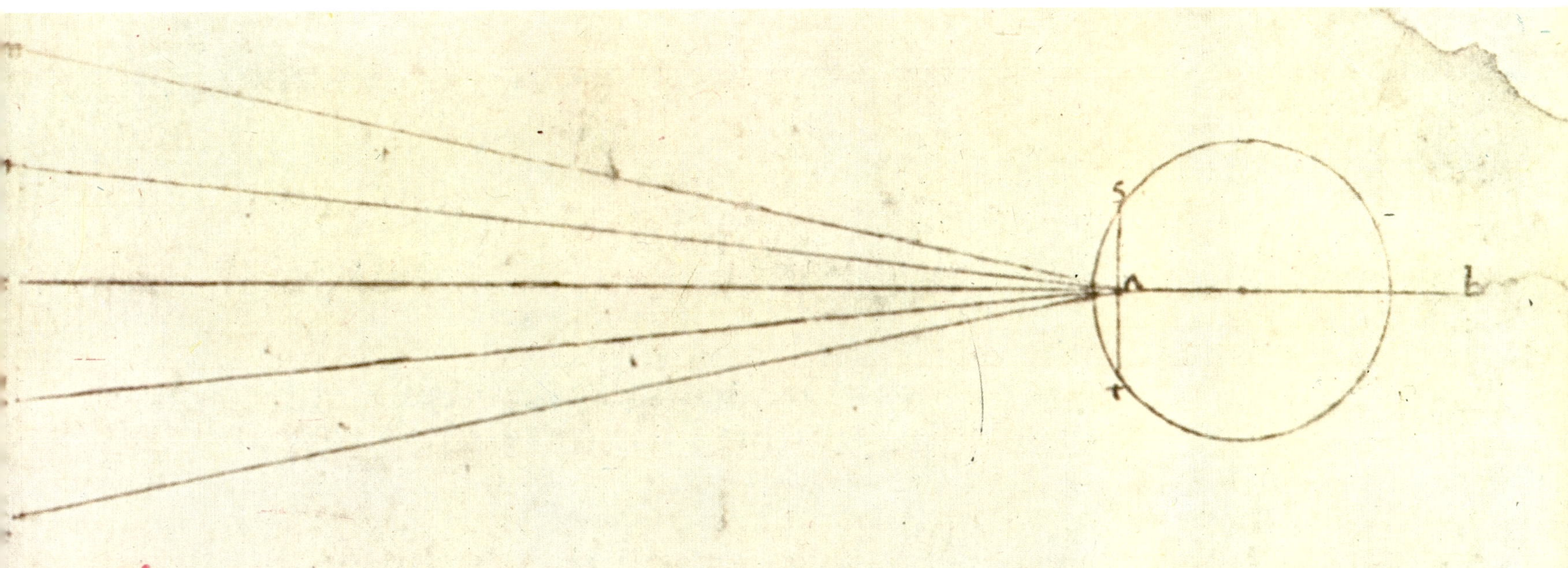

17

In che modo locchio vede le chose poste dinanzi

Pogniamo che quela palla fighurata di sopra sia la palla dellocchi e quela picola parte minore de la palla che divisa dalla linia s t sia la luce e tutte le chose spechiate sul mezo dello superficie della luce . subito si schorrono e vanno nella popilla passando per un certo omore cristallino cho non ne ochupa nella popilla chose che si dimostri alla luce E essa popilla riceve le chose dalla luce . immediate . le riferisse e porge allo intelletto . per la linia a . b . E sappi chella popilla non porge nessuna chosa perfetta mente allo intelletto overo senso chomune . se non quando le chose allei date . dalla luce si dirizano per la linia . a . b . sicchome vedi che fa la linia . c . e la che le linie . m . n . f . g . sieno vedute dalla popilla non sono chosi diritte . perche non si dirizano chella linia . a . b . E la pruova sie questa se questo ochio qui di sopra che vorra annumerare le tere poste li dinanzi cho uerra che locchio giri dalle ce ... alletteri . perche non le essere nobile se nolle dirizasi per la linia . a . b . sicchome fa la linia . c . a . / E tu le chose vedute mettono allochio ~~allochio~~ per linie piramidate ella punta di detta piramida fa termine e fine nel mezo della popilla chome di sopra e fighurato

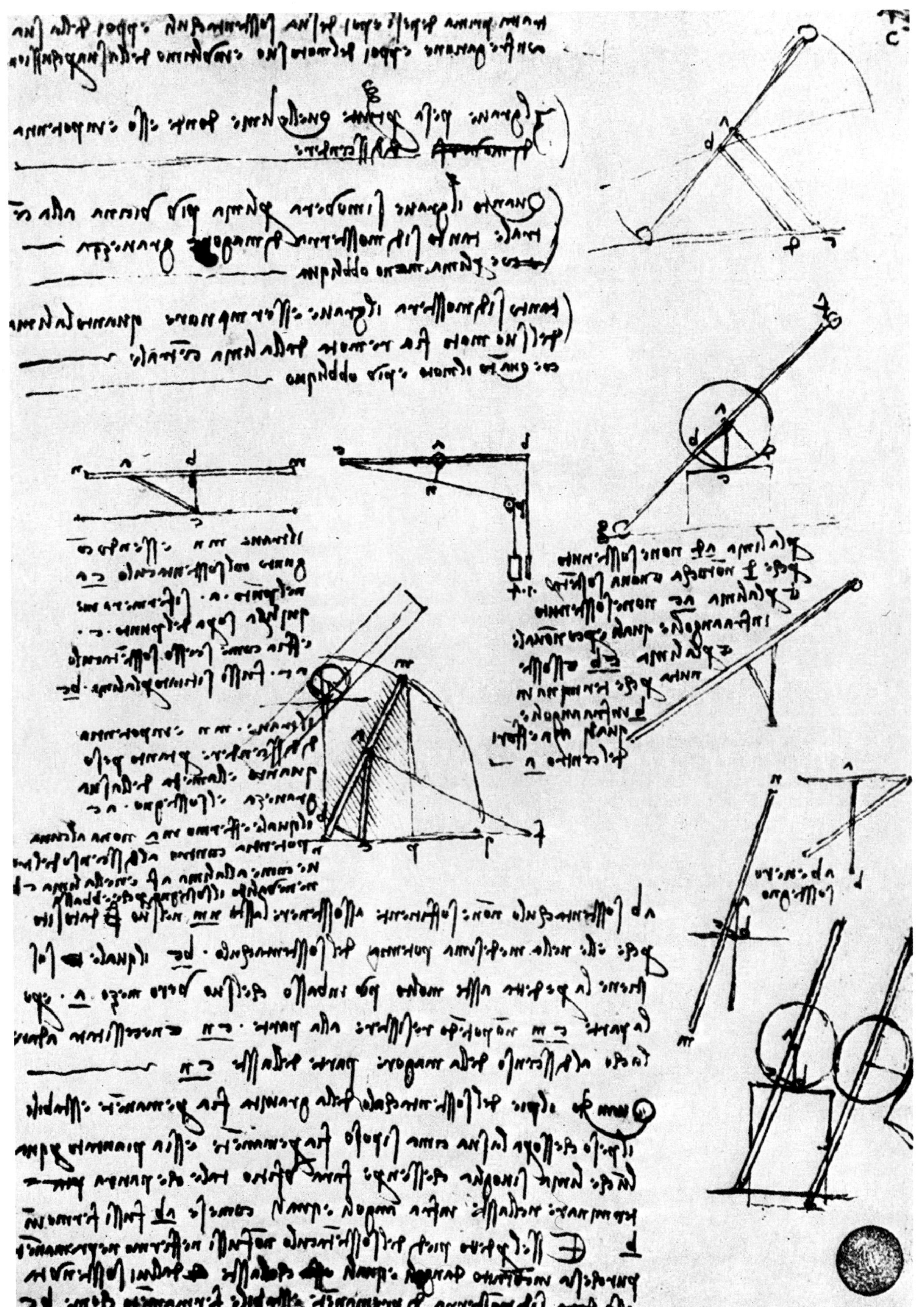

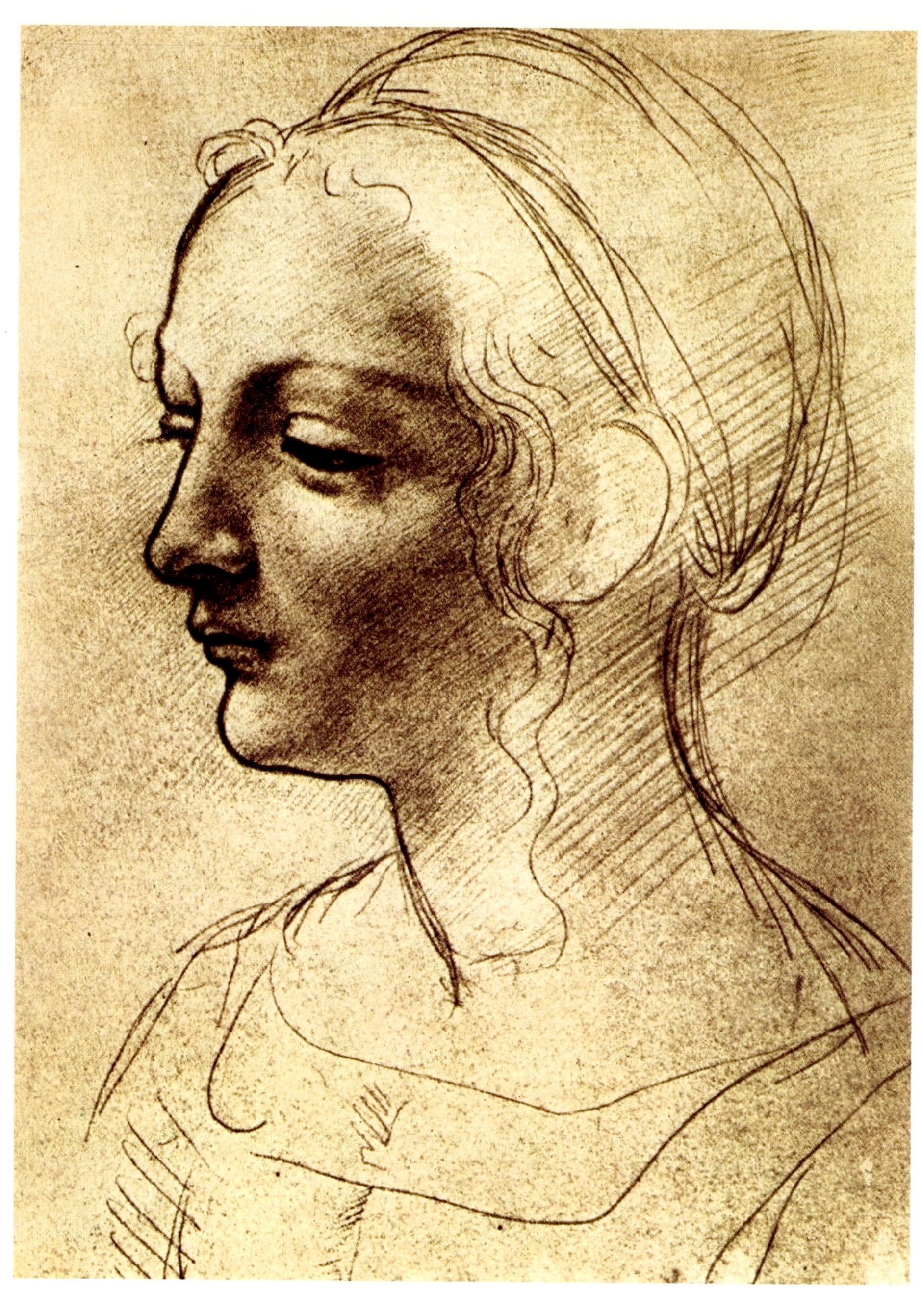

LVIII

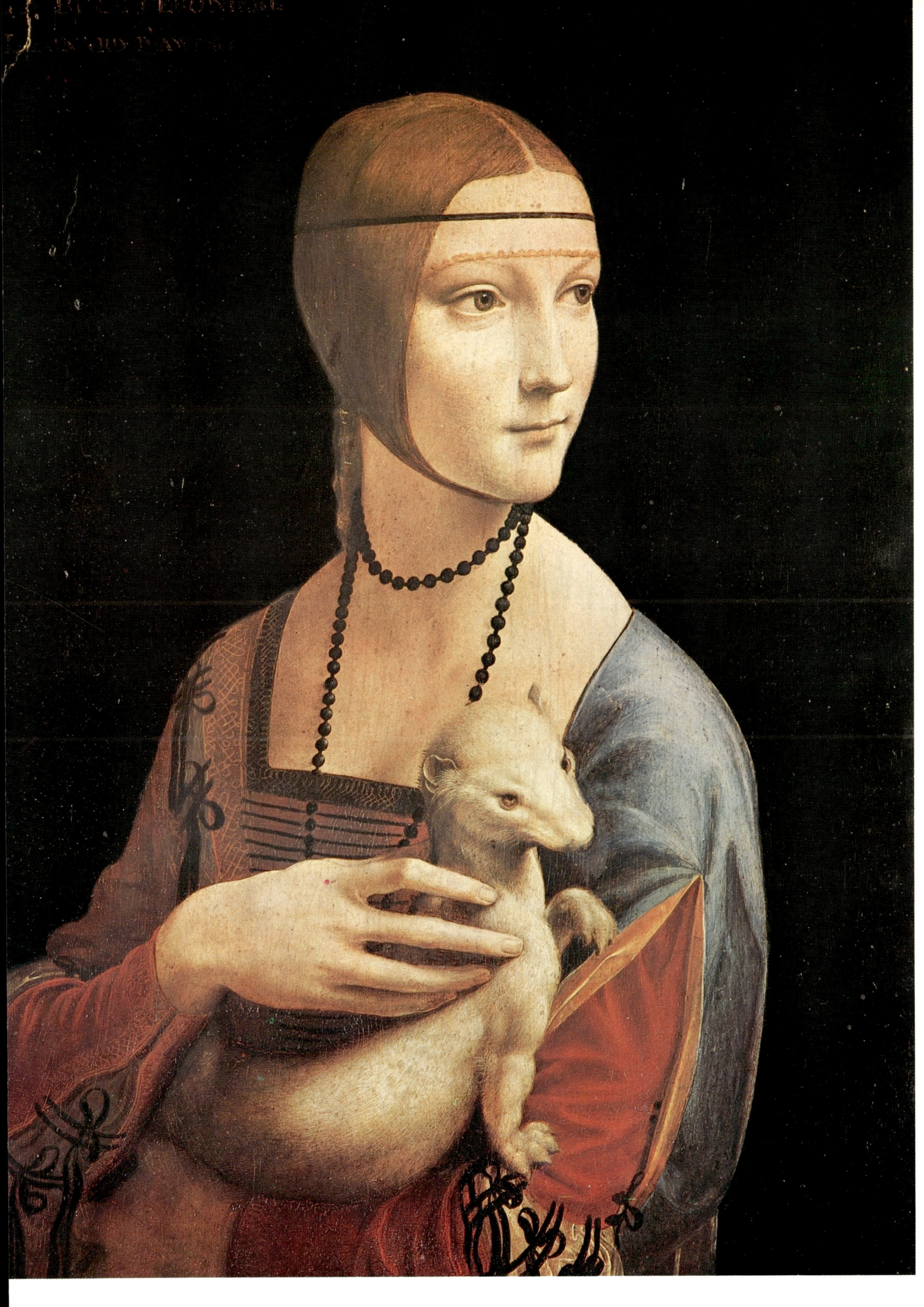

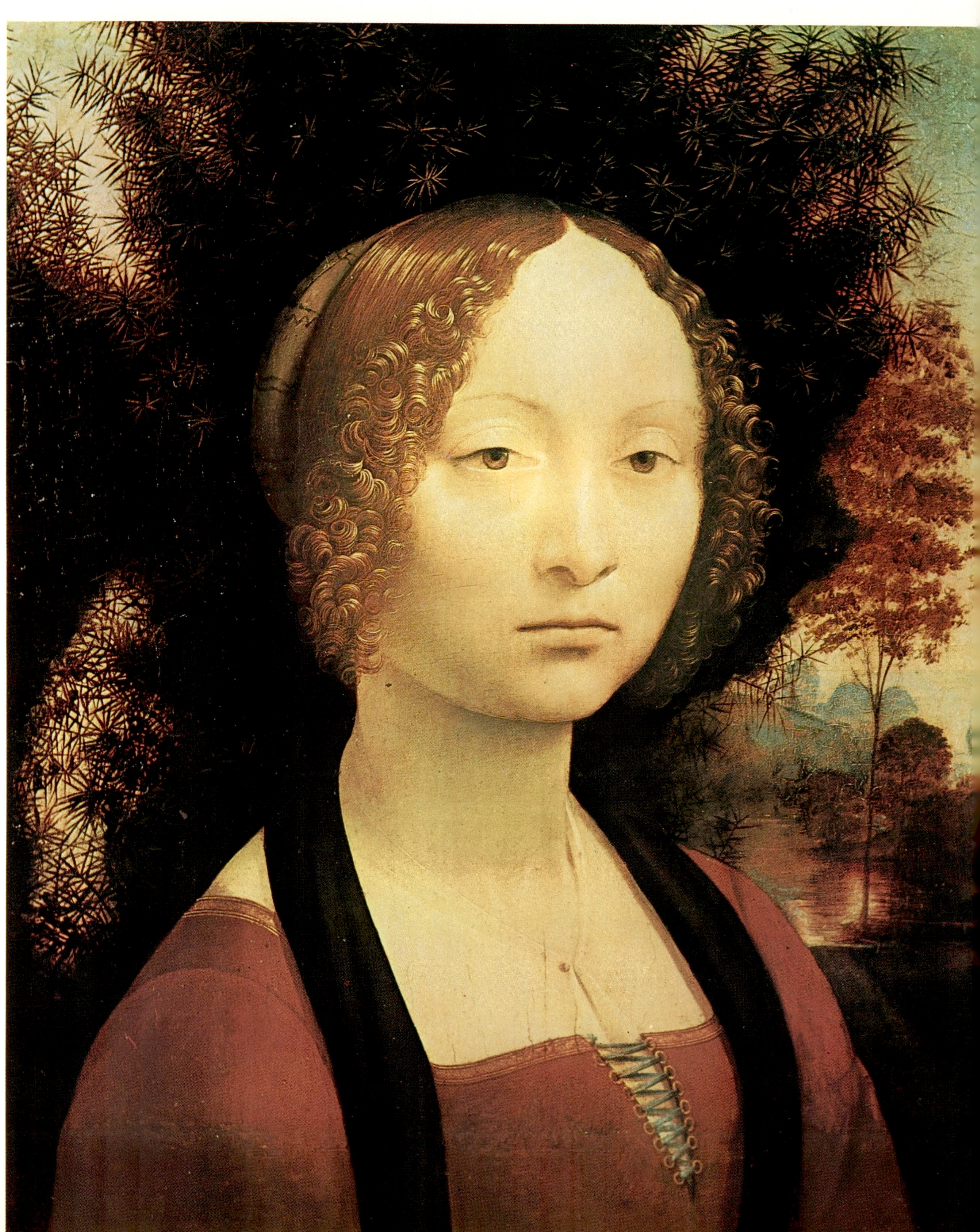

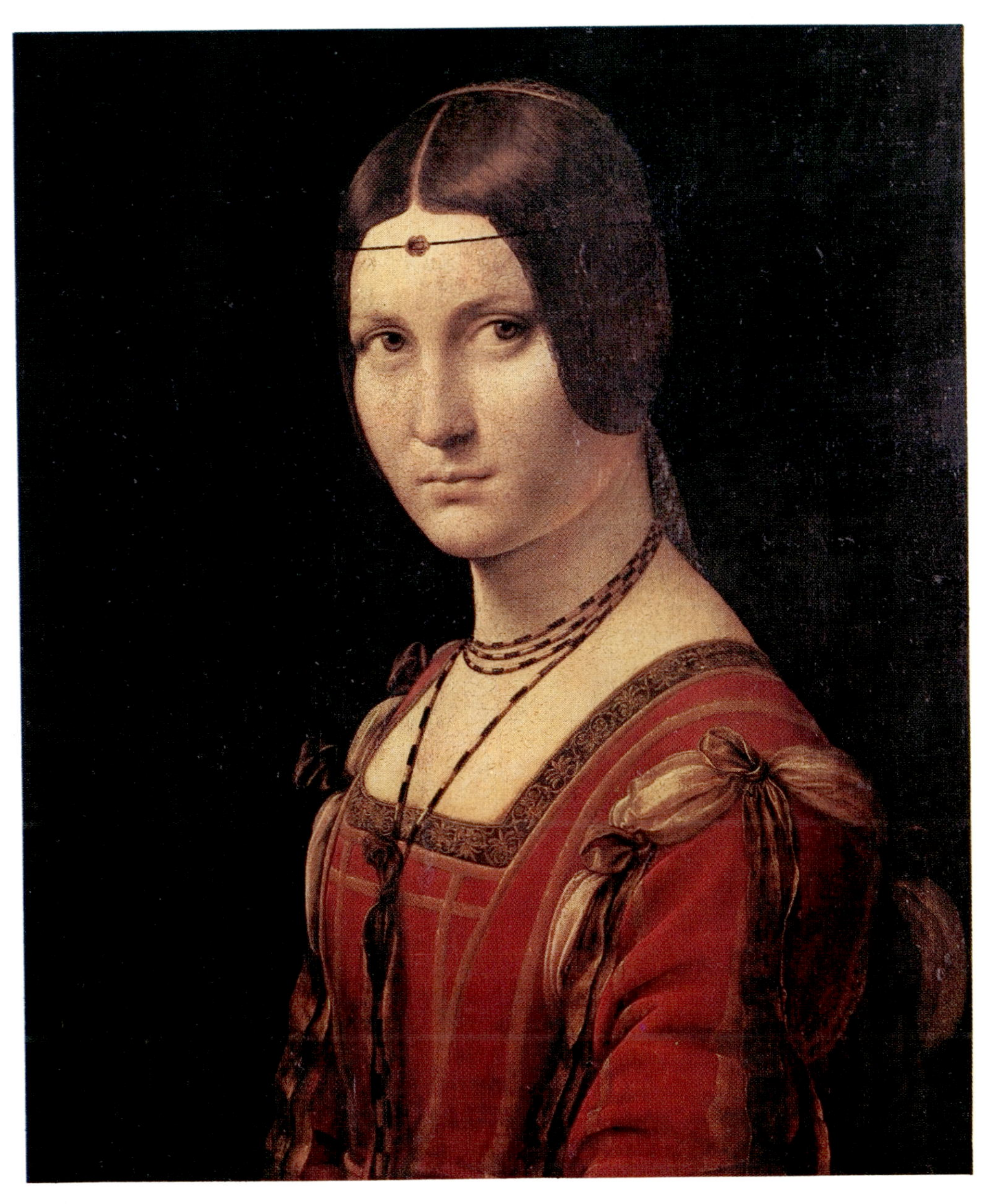

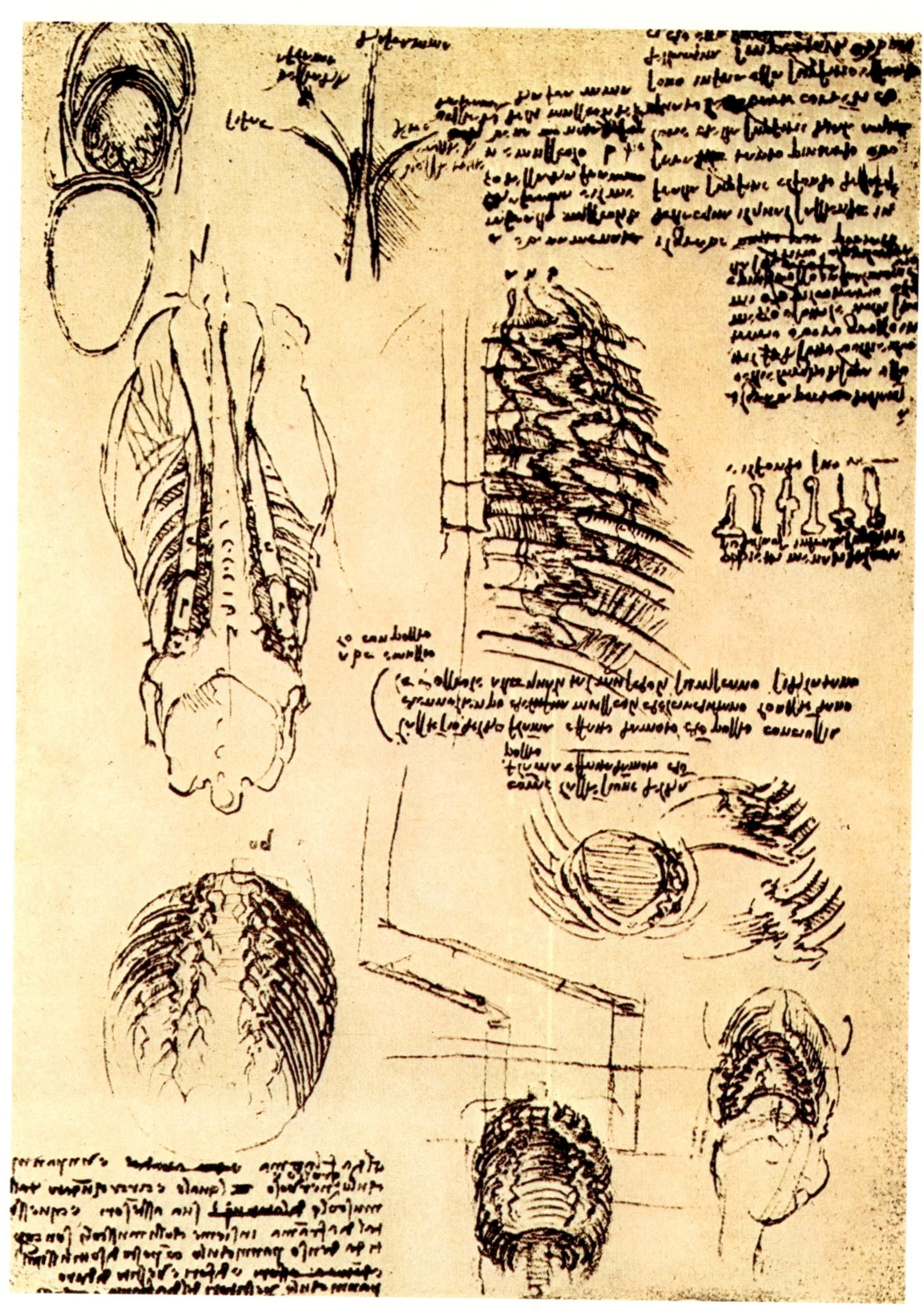

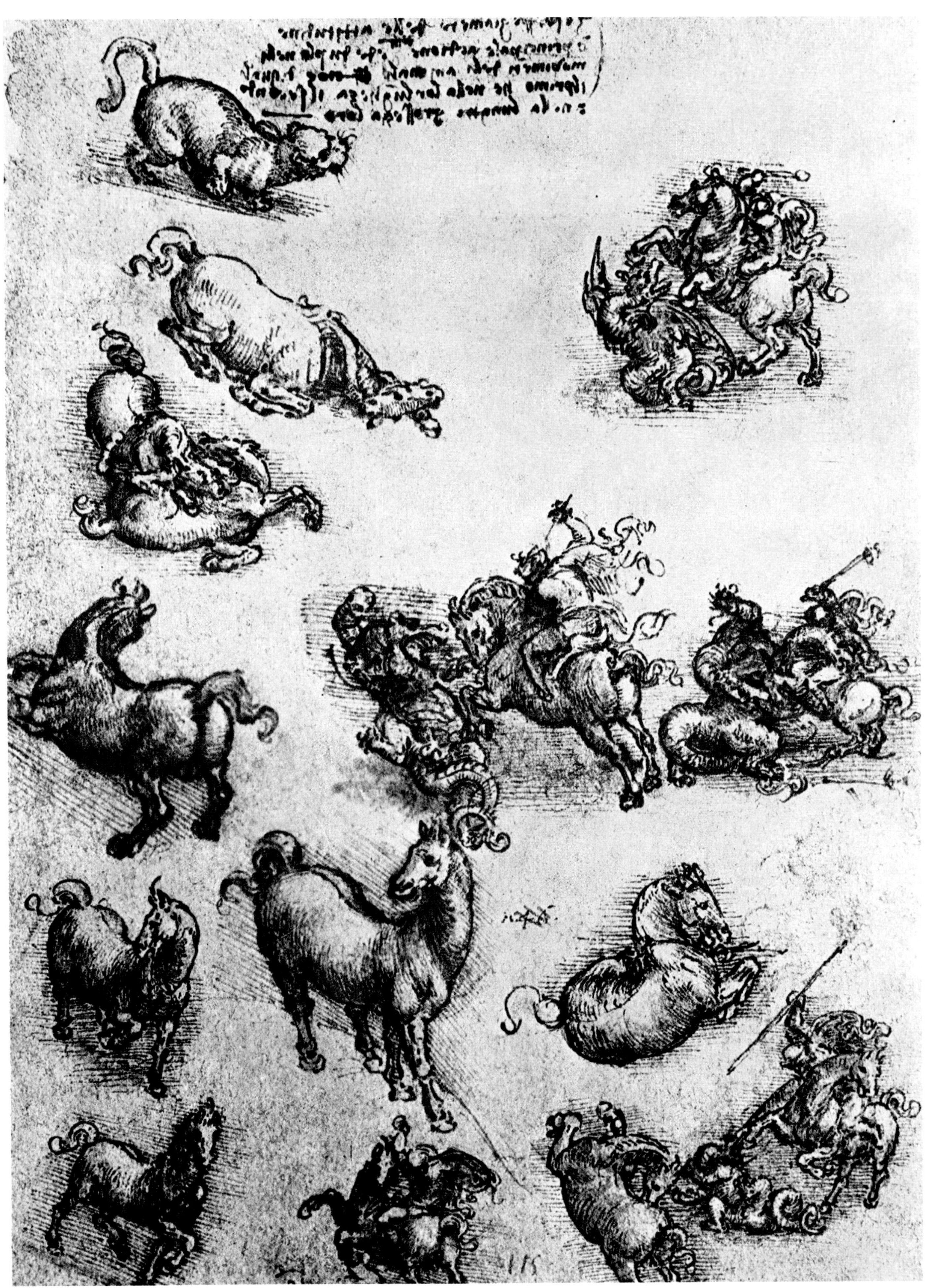

LXIII

Illustrations from the Picture Archives of Fabbri Editori, Milan
Printed in June 1978, at the graphic plant of Fabbri Editori - Milan, Italy